ARCTIC CHALLENGE

OUR LIFE IN AN ESKIMO VILLAGE WHILE ESTABLISHING THE FIRST HIGH SCHOOL ABOVE THE ARCTIC CIRCLE

Ruth Moline Eddy

Published by

The Book Garden
28 Bridge Street
Frenchtown, NJ 08825
Tel. 908-996-2022
Email: info@bookgarden.biz

Copyright © 2004 by Ruth Moline Eddy.
All rights reserved.

ISBN 0-9753109-0-9

Photos on pages 3, 15, 23, 29, 45, 61, 85, 97, 109, 135 and cover by Don Moline.
Photos on pages 51, 65, and 71, courtesy City of Kotzebue Historic Pictures Gallery.

Printed in the United States of America

All native persons referred to in this account are real but I have changed their names since I had no opportunity to get permission to use their true identity. The one exception is Martha Washington (really her name) who is a public figure having been featured in articles in National Geographic Magazine.

Kotzebue and the surrounding villages

It's the beauty that thrills me with wonder,
It's the stillness that fills me with peace.

>   Robert Service—
>   *The Spell of the Yukon*

CONTENTS

Editor's Note---1
Our Arrival—7
Why Alaska?—10
The Village of Kotzebue—17
Debbie in the Huskies' Den—25
The Big Event—27
Building the School---31
Living Conditions---36
Eskimo Housing—47
The Alaskan Working Dog---53
Tourists—63
Tundra and Mosquitoes—67
School Begins—73
Thanksgiving and Christmas—81
The Inevitable Illnesses---87
The Eskimo Language---93
Teaching the Children—99
Our First School Year Ends—105
Our Second School Year Begins—112
A Trip to the Lower States and a New Baby ---117
Summertime and a Visit from the U-2—120
Dishonesty Knows No Racial Barriers---124
Our Third Year—126
An Interesting Life---130
Wild Creatures of the Arctic—137
Going Home---140
An Update---142
Epilogue—147

Photos:

Ruth, Debbie and Don Moline—3
An Inupiat Eskimo—15
An Inupiat Eskimo woman—23
Friends school, church, bell tower and dormitory—29
A sod igloo with whalebone frame—45
Kotzebue Eskimo housing (about 1960)—51
Balto—59
After the hunt—61
Poverty is not pretty—65
The Tundra—71
Winter in Kotzebue—85
Eskimo children dressed for winter—97
The blanket toss—109
The midnight sun in Arctic Alaska—135

ARCTIC CHALLENGE

Editor's Note

While reading James Michener's novel, *Alaska*, I remembered that my sister, Ruth Moline Eddy, had spent some years in Arctic Alaska – establishing a school and teaching, as I recalled. I decided to contact her regarding her adventure, for two reasons. I was curious as to how some of Michener's observations compared with her first-hand experiences in this land, and also with the expectation that she would have some interesting tales to tell.

I was not disappointed. After reading a few of her narrations sent by e-mail I suggested that she write the story of her adventures in the Eskimo village of Kotzebue for everyone to enjoy. I offered to edit it. That was the catalyst she needed. What followed was an explosion of epistles.

I'm sure that reading her story will cause you to share my admiration for this lady who was undaunted by the challenge of this harsh difficult land in her dedication to improving the lives of the native Eskimos.

Bill Fleming

Ruth Moline Eddy

ARCTIC CHALLENGE

**Ruth, Debbie and Don Moline
in
Kotzebue, August 1959**

Ruth Moline Eddy

ARCTIC CHALLENGE

Ruth Moline Eddy

ARCTIC CHALLENGE

Our Arrival

We landed at the airport at Kotzebue, Alaska, on July 8, 1959 – my 30th birthday. We climbed into a pickup truck; our eleven month old daughter Debbie sat with me in the cab and my husband Don rode in the open back with our luggage. There were actually snowflakes in the air. Not a significant quantity, but I had never experienced snowflakes falling on my birthday before.

As we drove down the dirt road into town and I looked at the rows of unpainted plywood or metal shacks, I realized that life would indeed be different. There were no trees; just bush willows, some grass, and along the waterfront, fine gravel. There were also a few log buildings (the logs came from trees upstream on the Noatak River north of Kotzebue, I learned later). I saw two encouraging signs – the beautiful Brooks Range in the distance and the wonderful round rosy-cheeked faces of the curious children.

We had come to Kotzebue to establish a high school in the Arctic for Eskimo children. Upon arrival at our new home we were surprised to see

Ruth Moline Eddy

it was a two story house that would have been just the thing on an Iowa farm but conspicuously out of place in the Arctic. However, we appreciated the familiar look.

At this time Alaska had been a state for only six months, having been admitted to the Union as the 49th state on January 3, 1959. Since there had been no state government prior to this time there were only minimal services available to the natives. Although there were elementary schools in almost every village there was little opportunity for children to attend high school.

Prior to our establishing this school there was only one high school for Eskimos* – the Bureau of Indian Affairs school at Mt. Edgecumbe near Sitka. (The Eskimos are under the jurisdiction of the Bureau of Indian Affairs [BIA] even though they are not Indians.) Only the brightest and best were able to go to the BIA school so there really was no high school that the average Eskimo child could attend. Ours would be the first high school of any kind north of the Arctic Circle and it would be open to all with passing grades.

At Kotzebue a very basic curriculum had been set up by Quaker missionaries Paul and Patsy Miller but they needed someone certified to build

---

* The preferred designation today for these people seems to be "Inuit". However, we knew them as Eskimos and that is the term I shall use throughout this book.

ARCTIC CHALLENGE

these rudimentary beginnings into a full-fledged state-approved high school. This was our task.

This project proved to be quite a challenge; in fact almost every day seemed to present a new challenge in what was to us at this time a strange and forbidding but fascinating land.

However, within a year we had the school established, new building and all. At the close of our third year we graduated the first two high school students north of the Arctic Circle. Don was the principal and it was his privilege to sign the diplomas and hand them to the graduates. They had the gowns, mortar boards, a school choir singing, and the usual graduation fanfare. William Egan, governor of the state, had come a few weeks earlier to encourage those two graduates and challenge them with the fact that he, too, had graduated from a class of two and now he was governor of this great state. Subsequent graduations had larger classes, but none was as thrilling as the one on that day when history was made for the ordinary Eskimo teen.

This is the story of our experiences during the four years we spent on this project in this harsh land north of the Arctic Circle.

Ruth Moline Eddy

Why Alaska?

Why were we here and how did we get to be here? For the answer to those questions we must go back to my Taylor University days. Here I met Don Moline, my future husband and partner in this venture, while I was studying for my degree in social work.

Don's life is an incredible story in itself. He died in 1993 at the age of 60 of cancer. He had suffered from polio in his teens and at 19 years of age he had been given one chance in a hundred of living; no chance of ever walking again if he did live. He was in an iron lung and then in the hospital for almost nine months. Ironically, he who was never to walk again left his footprints on three continents and in many foreign lands. He was definitely a walking miracle.

Don's heart was in the Arctic when I met him; and when he was ready to go I agreed to this venture. We were now married with a baby daughter but I wasn't going to deprive him of his life's dream.

We found a means and a purpose in going on this adventure. However, we knew that going to

ARCTIC CHALLENGE

Alaska would be more than just an adventure. We knew there would be hardships but we were also very cognizant of the needs of the Eskimos. We heard that the Quaker Church was interested in establishing a high school for Eskimos in the Arctic and we applied for this project even though we were not Quakers. We felt this was a special calling when we, non-Quakers living over two thousand miles away, were chosen by the Quaker Church of California for such an awesome project. Before accepting us they had sent a representative to Michigan to talk with us and to visit our respective classrooms. We had then taken a battery of psychological tests. That was their only contact with us until we arrived in California for our send-off to Kotzebue.

A bit of background on this Quaker project: In 1885 a former missionary named Sheldon Jackson was appointed General Agent of Education for the territory of Alaska. He was charged with the task of bringing civilization to the native population. Jackson devised a plan to divide the territory of Alaska into regions, giving specified areas to designated religious denominations rather than have them compete with each other. Kotzebue was given to the Quakers. The Quakers, also known as Friends, first came to the Arctic in 1897 when Eskimo villages were still largely made up of sod igloos. These missionaries went from village to village, living among the people and learning to communicate with them.

How their efforts led to the rapid Christianizing of almost the entire northwest region of Arctic Alaska is a fascinating story.

When the Friends Church was being established in Kotezebue a number of missions were already in place. Their broad purpose, in keeping with the responsibility charged to Sheldon Jackson, was to bring the Eskimos out of "barbarism" into civilization. Civilization meant "literacy in English, cleanliness, industry and Christianity" – the virtually total transformation of native existence. In keeping with this objective each of these missions included an elementary school and a nursing station.

Robert and Carrie Samms, a newly married couple, arrived in Kotzebue in 1897 to establish the mission for the Friends Church. There they met Uyaraq, an Inupiat Eskimo who had been converted to Christianity and spoke fluent English. They and several other Quaker missionaries joined in a project that eventually led to the conversion of most of the Inupiat natives of the Kotzebue Sound region.

Their message was not immediately accepted. They were often harassed by drunks and shamans. These shamans, the powerful medicine men who kept the Eskimos in line with taboos, spells and rituals of all kinds were a major obstacle to their efforts. The missionaries confronted the shamans and by openly breaking their taboos and proving that no punishment followed, tried to discredit them. This met with limited success; the natives simply decided that the taboos did not apply to the white man.

It was Uyaraq who made the difference. When he who was an Inupiaq* himself, openly and deliberately broke the taboos and yet suffered no consequences, it effectively destroyed the credibility of the shamans. For this reason most Inupiat Eskimos were converted by other Inupiat. In contrast to the methods of the shamans the missionaries brought about real cures by the use of simple medications. In addition, the Samms treated the Eskimos with love and concern, something they had never gotten from the "white man" before. To further their acceptance of this "new God" was word from other native groups that missionaries had also brought them new hope and release from the tyranny of the evil spirits. This kind of good news spread rapidly.

Helge Ingstad in his book *Nunamuit* says, "It was above all the many evil spirits which occupied the Eskimo mind. In addition there were taboos and ceremonies which had to be rigidly observed. Life was certainly not simple".

* Inupiaq is the singular form, Inupiat is the plural.

Gravesites near Kotzebue surrounded by picket fences to impale evil spirits who would carry off their dead are a mute testimony to those beliefs.

The 1960's Kotzebue area Eskimo was remarkably different from the 1900 era Eskimo because of the early missionaries and their Christian teachings. Those who had gone before us had improved the native's lives so much that they expected nothing but good from us and we did our best not to disappoint.

By the time we arrived there was no longer any attempt made to enforce the religious boundaries set up by Sheldon Jackson. At that time (1959) the town had three small churches besides the Friends church - one Southern Baptist, one Assembly of God and the third one a Catholic church.

ARCTIC CHALLENGE

An Inupiat Eskimo

Ruth Moline Eddy

ARCTIC CHALLENGE

The Village of Kotzebue

During the first week we worked on school supplies that had been pre-ordered for us. More supplies would be coming when The Alaska Steamship Company's annual ship arrived. We also prepared a room upstairs for a contractor and his helper who would be arriving soon to build the school.

Our food supply would not arrive until the advent of the annual ship in July or August but the mission superintendent had left some staples and the Eskimos brought us fresh caribou and salmon. This food supply, ordered in June from a warehouse in Seattle, would consist of canned and boxed goods and staples such as flour and sugar. This would have to last us a year until the ship returned. We would be without fresh fruits and vegetables after the few crates of potatoes and apples we had ordered were used up. One year when choppy seas caused much of the flour to get wet our baked goods had a musty flavor. We finally gave some of this flavorful flour away for dog food.

Ruth Moline Eddy

Our arrival in early July was still the time of the midnight sun. It was light 24 hours a day, though the very latest hours were more like early dusk. The sun never set; it rolled along the horizon and then back up again. We had shades on our windows and had no difficulty sleeping, except when some of the young men played basketball too close to our house or a group of successful hunters got a bit too exuberant on the beach a block or two away. Since it didn't get really dark, there was activity all through the night although not at the same pace as during the more normal daylight hours.

Of the 1,200 residents of the village of Kotzebue only about 50 were non-natives. We soon got to know many of them. There were three or four nurses at the hospital and a doctor (occasionally two). There was a dentist and the elementary school principal and his son. Also the staff at the elementary school, mostly single ladies. Several other non-natives were employed at Bullock's shipping and fuel depot and at least one at the post office. There were non-native owners of local businesses such as Eckhardt's Trading Post, Rotman's general store and Hanson's Trading Company which also carried groceries. There were also the clergymen of the three small churches and their families. Then there were a few non-natives whose gainful activity, if any, was not apparent.

ARCTIC CHALLENGE

In the early days Kotzebue was not the largest Eskimo village in Arctic Alaska – Noorvik was. Noorvik was the center of Bureau of Indian Affairs management for the Kobuk region. However, by the time we arrived in 1959 Kotzebue was the largest Eskimo village north of the Arctic Circle in Alaska with its 1,200 inhabitants. It most likely was the advent of the airplane and the fact that Kotzebue was far more accessible by both air and sea that caused its rapid growth. When we were there the number of dogs exceeded the number of humans, but due to the snowmobile there are now not nearly as many dogs. The current human population is about 3,600, made up primarily of Inupiat Eskimos.

Kotzebue stands about 30 miles above the Arctic Circle on a peninsula jutting into Kotzebue Sound, named for the German explorer OttoVon Kotzebue. The sound leads into the Chukchi Sea and the Arctic Ocean. The Kobuk, Noatak and Selawik rivers flow into the sound near Kotzebue, enabling boat traffic to carry cargo and residents to the local villages located on these rivers. Large ships do come to the area but must remain out at sea because of the shallower waters of the Continental Shelf. Goods are lightered in. Lightering is the transfer of freight to a smaller vessel that can go up to the shipping docks to unload. At Kotzebue the larger freighters cannot come any closer than 12 miles out. It is just too shallow for those vessels.

There were no roads leading in or out of town (and there are none today) except for a one-mile stretch from the town to the airport, due to the instability of the tundra – a flat, treeless, windswept expanse which completely surrounds the area except for the sea.

Typical of the Arctic, the winters are long and cold – the average low temperature during January is 12 degrees below zero. There is ice in the sound from early October until June or July. The summers are short and cool. The average high temperature in July is 58. The record extremes are -52 and 85.

Kotzebue with its topography of gravel beaches and something resembling grassy fields just beyond the beaches, is not the most picturesque spot in Alaska. But in mid spring we did have flowers. They were abundant on the sloping hills toward the airfield – some years like a carpet – low to the ground but thick and colorful. Inland it was mostly fireweed; something like the vagabond purple loosestrife the Nature Conservancy is seeking to eradicate. It had a tall brilliant spire of blooms and often grouped itself into what could resemble a fire.

A few of our other villages were located on small steep hills covered with large evergreen trees. Those were the picturesque ones, but they

ARCTIC CHALLENGE

had drawbacks as well – living inland in the wooded, hilly villages had some definite disadvantages. First there was the problem of having to climb the very steep slopes that led to the river, the main source of transportation. It was especially difficult carrying supplies up these hills when the smaller ships lightering their goods from the freighter out in the bay arrived. Eventually someone made life easier by building a track up the hillside. Then a kind of miniature railroad car was built which could be pulled up this track. It certainly beat carrying crates. Eventually it was motorized. The other drawback of these inland villages was the mosquitos. But more about that later.

Ruth Moline Eddy

ARCTIC CHALLENGE

An Inupiat Eskimo Woman

Ruth Moline Eddy

ARCTIC CHALLENGE

Debbie in the Huskies' Den

I had a frightening experience soon after our arrival in this new land. We had been in Kotzebue just one full day when we had to have our typhoid shots. Debbie was given too strong a dose and I found her in her crib pale and limp as a rag doll. I gathered her up quickly and ran, carrying her, to the native hospital two blocks away. The jostling as I ran apparently shocked her back into full circulation and she was almost back to normal when the doctor looked at her. A week later she had the second shot. She was given only a half dose and that resulted in no problems.

Another heart-stopping incident involving Debbie took place when we had been in Kotzebue only a few weeks. I was outdoors talking with some Eskimo ladies with Debbie playing nearby. Suddenly one of the ladies began to scream. There was one-year-old Debbie in the middle of a dog stake-out. This was very alarming because Eskimos did not treat their dogs kindly – they were not pets and their dispositions reflected that. I cautiously and fearfully approached Debbie and she simply walked out, with the dogs paying absolutely no attention to her – something like Daniel in the lion's den.

Debbie's first reaction to the Eskimo children was to be somewhat frightened. When they came to our house they would come in small groups and just stand near the door, looking at her and saying nothing. That was strange behavior to Debbie. They were fascinated with her toys but didn't quite know how to relate to this blue-eyed, light-haired little creature. The Eskimo children had almost no toys. Debbie's tricycle and little red wagon were special attractions and when they got to know her they loved to pull her in the wagon.

The Big Event

On our 8th day in Kotzebue the Quarterly Meeting began – the biggest event of the year! This was a church convention when people from all ten villages in the Kobuk River region came to Kotzebue for six days of meetings and services.

This odd practice of calling an annual meeting The Quarterly Meeting needs some explaining. It is due to a tradition of the Quakers that goes back to eighteenth century England – when the Society of Friends held their important business conventions four times a year. When they later changed their meetings to annual affairs they continued to call them Quarterly Meetings.

So the Quarterly Meeting of the Quakers is now an annual event and in our case it was used each year as an opportunity to bring the Eskimos together to try to eradicate tribal animosity. This gathering was a phenomenon of great significance. Eskimos were not known for getting along with the Indians; inland Eskimos claimed that the coastal Eskimos were different people, and the Eskimos in the villages within the Kobuk region had a clan-like mentality. They did not like their young people marrying those from other villages. The very earliest Quaker missionaries wrote of feuds and occasional physical violence. As these missionaries went from village to village, showing compassion, providing medical aid, and converting them, many of the Eskimos formed a common bond – their new faith.

This Quarterly Meeting was a wonderful thing – I was awed by it. Services were almost entirely in Eskimo with speakers from every village and singing groups from every village. Eskimo singing is very different from ours – strong and nasal and somewhat harsh, but it was heartfelt and joyous and a very moving experience.

There was some English spoken at that mainly Eskimo gathering. There were a few Eskimos who felt comfortable enough to speak briefly before a group in their acquired language. Harold Beck the mission superintendent also spoke, as did Don, but both of these used an interpreter, or interrupter as Don called them. The last night of this convention was the grand finale. It lasted until 3 AM. It seemed everyone had to say one more thing or sing one more song.

ARCTIC CHALLENGE

Friends high school, church, bell tower and dormitory

Ruth Moline Eddy

Building the School

While the Eskimo folks were enjoying the Quarterly Meeting two men came to Kotzebue almost unnoticed. They were Charlie Warren and Les Blair from Yorba Linda, CA. Les was the contractor who was to oversee the work of building the school and Charlie was his assistant. The convention ended, as previously mentioned, at three o'clock Monday morning. A few hours later the bulldozer from the local shipping company was digging an enormous hole for the foundation of the school and attached apartment. I do not know the dimensions but the building would contain three classrooms, a larger library/assembly room, and a three bedroom apartment for the principal. Later, when the school was completely finished we would move into the attached apartment (since Don was the principal) and another couple who joined us would move into the "big house".

Ordinarily a building this size would be placed on pilings because of the permafrost. The Eskimos were still laughing about a large garage the Army Corps of Engineers erected at one of the

Ruth Moline Eddy

DEW (Distant Early Warning) line stations that simply collapsed in the middle. The ground was what is called ice-rich; the concrete disturbed the permafrost and it began melting. Eventually it became soft enough to sink a bit. Any Eskimo could have told them it wouldn't work, and possibly they did, which would make the situation even more laughable. The school, however, was built on what was really gravel beach. In fact, the men turned right around and used the gravel they had bulldozed out to mix with the cement for the foundation.

When they were done with that they dug a well for a limited supply of water, not enough for flush toilets but sufficient for washing just like in our "big house". The source of the water at the big house was snow and rain caught in a cistern; this was from underground. The well water was somewhat salty but not like water directly from an ocean. It had gone through the beach gravel first, and though not fit for drinking it was suitable for washing.

About the time the contractors were ready for the framing of the building but were waiting for the lumber I was up on a rise near the airport and saw a black spot on the horizon. It was the annual ship anchored about twelve miles from shore. It carried the wood for building the school as well as our usual supplies. In three days the wood was unloaded and immediately the forms were put up for the cement work. Our barrels of personal belongings arrived two days after that, and then our groceries.

About this time Don, Debbie, Charlie (the contractor's assistant) and a young man from Noorvik all got sick – dysentery accompanied by fever. However, the work went on. It was the time of the midnight sun so everyone put in long hours. It was now August and that is usually the rainy month. But fortunately the weather continued to be dry and warm (60's to 70). In two days these few men had the cement work completed and were ready for framing.

It was now 22 days since the ship came in and we were finally getting the last of the boxes of clothes for the Eskimos and books for the school. We also got some more help. An elderly couple visiting the Arctic stayed and helped me with feeding the workers and caring for Debbie. With all those people in and out of the house the cistern ran dry. This meant that some of the men had to quit working on the school and go out to the lagoon to haul in barrels of water. Two days later it began to rain and the work stopped.

While the freighter was being unloaded yet another Californian arrived. Ron Woodward, a tall blond young man, came to join us as a teacher and also the overseer of the Eskimo church. Ron was to live upstairs in the "big house" while we lived downstairs until the new apartment was ready. Ten days after his arrival he got "the bug" (dysentery). Welcome to Eskimoland, Ron! A few days later he performed a wedding and buried the first of a number of babies to die from complications of measles.

We were in our seventh week in Alaska and had already learned to depend on Joe and Mollie. Joe was a huge, jolly, rather crude Eskimo with a plain and equally amiable wife. They came to see us on the day of our arrival and dropped in frequently. Joe had his summer tent pitched a short distance behind our house. He was notorious for all the "stuff" that always surrounded his abode – washing machine (run by kerosene), lots of 50 gallon drums for storage, equipment of all kinds, skins, anything there was a chance he might use. Someone gave us some salmon and Mollie came by and cleaned it the efficient Eskimo way with her ulu – a half-circle knife with a handle on top. She made Don some mukluks, got him some muskrat skins and later made him a gorgeous parka, beadwork and all. Eventually she made all of us at least two parkas and several pairs of mukluks.

Molly and Joe appeared to be true partners and to really enjoy each other's company. Molly giggled at the things Joe said, for instance, and Joe had a very special look of tenderness when he talked to her. This was quite typical of the marriages of the older Eskimos; the men treated

ARCTIC CHALLENGE

their wives kindly and the wives respected their men. Possibly the hardships of Arctic life brought this about. The marriages of the younger people were not always so stable, especially if the husband went away to Fairbanks or a mining camp to work, or was involved in the heavy consumption of alcohol which sometimes took place when an Eskimo had money to spend. Divorce, which was once a rarity, was becoming more common.

Back to the building: On August 22 the work stopped due to the rain but two days later the men were able to resume. The framework had gone on a week earlier and now in one day the rafters for the roof went up and the roofing was put on the next day. This was possible because of the many volunteer helpers we had, some of them no more than 10 years old. The bubble gum crew, we called them. We had every confidence the building would withstand the Arctic winds with all that bubble gum holding it together.

After another two-day rain delay the siding went on. These were wooden panels and while they were being placed, Don wired the entire building. He also stayed up quite late doing things like cutting up caribou that had been brought in and on several occasions he went fishing. I was kept busy baking bread and pies, and grinding up the caribou for hamburger.

Ruth Moline Eddy

Living Conditions

We were usually well supplied with fish and game that Don would catch or shoot locally. He enjoyed hunting so this was not a problem. We were also able to pick some wild blueberries (not exactly like the blueberries we were accustomed to) and we were able to freeze those. I baked all bread from scratch and was able to make pies with canned fruits. So we were never hungry – we did not have to resort to ingesting Eskimo fare such as whale blubber or seal oil. But we did on occasion politely and sparingly taste these and a few other such "delicacies". Generally, the meat from the four footed animals was good, as was the fish. And I learned from the Eskimos how to make a really tasty caribou stew. Potlucks were really interesting, but I'll discuss that in another episode.

Water supply and sewage disposal were, at best, crude. Most of the time we had water running out of our faucets. It came from a cistern which collected water from rain or melting snow on the roof as I explained earlier. This water could not be used for drinking but could be used for such things as washing. Sometimes, if rains were scarce or the thaws were late, it was necessary to resort to whatever sources of water we could find.

Drinking water came from another source – a fresh water lagoon about a mile away. Not having the means to haul but a small amount in the liquid form, we cut ice from this lagoon in October and November and hauled these blocks to an ice house. We had a gasoline-powered circular saw; most of the Eskimos cut theirs with hand saws. The ice had to be cut when it was about a foot thick. Thinner blocks meant surplus cutting and loading; thicker blocks were too hard to cut and move. These blocks were then placed on the sturdy ancient mission truck and hauled to the ice house adjoining our residence. We tried to store enough to last an entire year.

The lagoon water was not safe to drink without treatment. Each of our families had a 50 gallon metal drum with a faucet at the bottom. Two or three ice blocks (maybe four) from the lagoon would be placed in the barrel to thaw and Clorox was added. Occasionally the barrel was cleaned out to get rid of the bit of debris that was a natural part of lagoon water.

Doing the laundry was quite a chore. We had an old ringer washing machine that we filled with buckets of water and then we hung the wet laundry throughout the house (no dryers).

Ruth Moline Eddy

During the short summer, clothes were hung on lines outside. One day while hanging clothes I found daisies growing and blooming – exactly the same kind that grew in the fields of Michigan except they were of short stature. The flowers were normal size but the stems and leaves were only two or three inches high – an adaptation on the part of a plant as though it knew somehow that it could not waste precious time producing a sizeable plant; it had to go right to the flower and seed-producing process. This was true of other plants in the Arctic. We'd probably call them stunted. I've seen trees and plants use the same survival techniques during a couple of summer droughts in Michigan. They would bear flowers and fruits very prematurely as though to say, "I may die, but there will be seeds for new plants".

The real hazard was human wastes. Flush toilets were unknown and impossible to have without wells. The white folks had honey buckets – 5 gallon buckets with a seat built over them. When full they were carried outside to a previously dug hole with a cover over it. Most Eskimos had far less than this – some used the great out-of-doors (modesty was not a high priority). That first winter, when it got really cold, I would hear a child cry and yell very loudly every night. I wondered if he was being spanked outdoors, which would be a rarity for an Eskimo child. I discovered in time that he was placed

ARCTIC CHALLENGE

outside for potty time and his poor little bottom would sting from the cold, and so he yelled in protest.

Adding to our enjoyment of this segment of Arctic living were the wastes of 1200+ dogs. You can understand why we often appreciated the wind-driven snows that carried everything off to Siberia. The Eskimos used to say we really didn't get a lot of snow; we just traded it back and forth with the Soviets. We were actually just a couple of hundred miles from there. On a particularly clear morning we could see Soviet airplanes as they rose into the air from a landing strip located on the edge of the mainland.

We soon realized that Alaska was a land of contrasts: the vast flat tundra surrounded by majestic mountains and – in summer – bathed in the glow of the fiery midnight sun. Utterly drab colorless homes standing in stark contrast with the gorgeous ornate parkas and mukluks (Eskimo boots), the men's being the most colorful. The beauty of the young people contrasted to the women who aged quickly and dramatically after giving birth to a few children – the effect of the harshness of survival in an unforgiving climate. And easy laughter that was a coping mechanism for deep superstitious fears.

Yes, at times it really was cold. When living at "the big house" a wet washcloth dropped on the floor would freeze in a short period of time.

Ruth Moline Eddy

During one winter I spent a portion of a number of days huddled next to an oil stove trying to keep warm. I could have worn my fur parka indoors but to me that was far too cumbersome. Besides, fur parkas can't be washed. Older Eskimo women had cloth covers they put over theirs for working but these were for the long parkas that went to their ankles. I was too young for those. Couldn't have my students think I was an old woman. I had one short "inside" parka (inside meaning with fur turned in) but it, too, did not have a removable outer covering. It had a lovely blue corduroy exterior with fancy trim. But since I wasn't gutting whales and seals or caribou like the Eskimo women; they didn't make a work parka for me.

In our second year temperatures of -40 and even -50 were more prolonged than usual. We were then living in our new apartment adjacent to the school and the floors were warmer because there was a basement. But when the temperature dipped below -20, frost crept across the floor near the walls and formed on the nails in the wall panels. At -20 our metal roof would emit a loud "pop" as it contracted.

The cold winters created some special problems even for the Eskimos. When a death occurred in mid-winter it was impossible to bury the body. The solidly frozen ground would be totally resistant to efforts to use a pick and shovel to dig a grave. The solution was to store the body in a shed – a veritable deep freeze where it would be perfectly preserved until the ground was again amenable to digging.

However, we were quite comfortable most of the time. Our mukluks, made of caribou skins with the fur side toward the feet, combined with heavy socks, kept our feet warm and we wore those just about all winter. The parkas did their job, too. The wonderful thing about them was the wolf ruff. It was made of wolf fur because that animal's fur repels the freezing of breath on it for the longest period of time. When the wind begins to blow, you pull that ruff forward and it projects far enough that the wind and cold cannot reach your face. It closes over the face, almost hiding it, but you can still see straight ahead. I would not recommend it in heavy traffic areas.

Another unique kind of parka was the mother's parka. It looked just like any other but there was extra room in the shoulder area. The mother, usually with help, hoisted the baby on her back with its head even with mom's neck. There was an air pocket there under the parka and I've never known of a baby of any age to suffocate. The baby was warm as toast and comfortable on mom's back. A sash kept the baby from slipping out of place.

A few of the older Eskimos would wear fur parkas all year long. In summer they would open them, fan themselves with them, and proclaim that it was hot as California. Meanwhile, oily perspiration (from seal oil they drank) appeared on their faces. The younger people, however, were only too happy to shed their parkas and dress more like people "stateside". In fact, some of them were quite underdressed in the wintertime much to the consternation of the public health workers.

The cold was responsible for some interesting natural phenomena as well. One was the aurora borealis – the northern lights which you have heard of. It was sometimes quite spectacular, covering much of the sky. Eskimo legend explained the changing, jumping lights as the activity of spirits having a wonderful time playing a game of kicking a walrus head around. Today's Eskimos are more interested in a scientific explanation. The other phenomenon was related to ice crystals high in the atmosphere. We were looking over towards the bay one morning when we saw a village out on the ice. Don recognized it as the village of Candle. We knew it had to be a kind of mirage like one sees on desert sands. It was indeed; only this was a reflection of a real place. It was a rare occurrence, and quite amazing. We never saw it again.

Another thrilling sight was the break-up of the ice in Kotzebue Sound. Some years it broke up and went out to sea within 24 hours and other years it took several days. One year the wind was blowing toward Kotzebue and the ice piled up on the beach just a few feet from homes and stores. The ice was several stories high with many individual pieces being taller than a man. The sound was what first alerted us – like a million ice cubes clinking in glasses of iced tea. It was a pleasant sound in a very dangerous situation.

Ruth Moline Eddy

ARCTIC CHALLENGE

**A sod igloo with whalebone frame;
Debbie standing on top and brother Jerry (born
at the end of our second year in the Arctic) in
the foreground**

(Igloo built by the airlines as a tourist attraction
but quite authentic in detail)

Ruth Moline Eddy

ARCTIC CHALLENGE

Eskimo Housing

It seems to be a fairly common impression that Eskimos lived in "igloos" – round structures made of blocks of ice. Igloo is the Eskimo name for *shelter*. Round igloos could be made of ice, snow, animal skins, sod or stone. Sod igloos were common in Kotzebue in earlier days but were almost nonexistent by the time we were there. The only ice igloo I have ever seen was one made by our students to educate their teachers.

Ice igloos do exist but in Alaska they are not homes. They are temporary shelters for those caught out in a storm in the winter. Before the government hospital was established in Kotzebue, women who had children born in winter usually went out to an ice igloo to give birth. That was at least partly because of the practice of destroying baby girls if a family already had several. Boys became hunters and therefore were worth keeping; "surplus" girls were left behind to freeze to death. This practice, as far as I know, no longer exists, thanks to the influence of the missionaries.

Ruth Moline Eddy

There are accounts of ice or snow igloos used as semi-permanent homes by some groups of Eskimos in Northern Canada and they are called winter snow houses. If you wonder why they don't melt from warmth in the interior of the structure it's because the heat generated inside the igloo was actually quite meager. It would come from the burning of a small amount of whale blubber or seal oil and was not enough to melt the snow blocks kept frozen by the extreme temperatures outside. Eskimos would wear most of their layers of clothes day and night, taking them off only for a very occasional clean-up time. They needed very little external heat.

The sod igloos were built partially below ground level with a wood or whale bone frame. Sod blocks were rounded about the frame similar to the way the ice structures were built. The sod igloos were not too different from the sod homes used on the western plains in the lower states except for their being rounded. They were dark and cool in the summer, dark and warm in the winter. Yes, sod igloos had become a rarity but there was one near our house that had been constructed by the airlines as a tourist attraction and as far as I could tell it was quite authentic.

As I mentioned, the Kotzebue Eskimos lived mostly in unpainted plywood or metal shacks. There were a few new homes built while we were there, most of these by couples in their late

ARCTIC CHALLENGE

thirties or older. Usually it meant that the husband worked in Fairbanks and was the kind who could hang on to his money. Those homes were made of plywood and were larger than the original homes, having three or maybe even four rooms. The older homes often had a shed-like entry way attached to one or two rooms. Walls were made of whatever materials could be found – usually wood or tin. Often beds (or just piles of furs for sleeping) lined a couple of the walls. Sometimes sheets were hung to serve as dividers. Some families had chairs and a table; others had furs and skins on which to sit when there really wasn't room for a table. Often there were as many as 6 to 8 people living in a one or two room house. No wonder camping out during the brief summer was so eagerly anticipated.

A few younger families were starting to put more windows in their homes, even painting the inside of their houses a bit, in an effort to make them more attractive. Generally, however, windows did not hold off the cold too well, so they were small and few in number. Painting the inside of these small dark, crudely built houses was really not worthwhile since it would be hardly noticeable.

As crowded as these homes were, they often became even more so when someone in the family got married and brought the new spouse home to live. Speaking of marriage, I did not see one church wedding and heard of very few during our four years there. Usually they took place at the bride or groom's home, at the mission house or at the office of the justice of the peace. The couple would dress up specially for the occasion but not in formal wedding attire as we know it. The ceremonies were very brief and were usually attended only by witnesses or close friends; sometimes even family members did not attend. Nor were they followed by large celebrations. Marriages often were only a legal statement of what had already taken place.

Perhaps the lack of fanfare has to do with the older custom of not marrying until the intended wife could prove her fertility by producing a child. Children were considered a necessity for the care of the parents when they grew too old to hunt for their own food and clothing. However, by this time (the 1960's) the prerequisite of being certain that a young woman could bear children was pretty much a thing of the past. Generally there was no official honeymoon or trip away from home, nor were there immediate plans for obtaining their own homes. After the wedding most couples returned to live in the home of the parents of either the bride or the groom. This was always a bit astonishing to me since these homes were already so overcrowded. Young couples were simply too poor to acquire their own homes.

ARCTIC CHALLENGE

Kotzebue Eskimo Housing (about 1960)

Ruth Moline Eddy

ARCTIC CHALLENGE

The Alaskan Working Dog

We quickly grew accustomed to the howling of the dogs, which happened mostly during the months when there was actually some darkness. Huskies generally do not bark; they howl like wolves. They were not easily disturbed, but if one of them was disturbed, it would begin a long, crescendo-like howl which was immediately joined by most of the other 1200 dogs in the village. Remarkably, after a few long soulful howls, usually all of them stopped at the same time as though on cue.

As I mentioned, Eskimos did not treat their sled dogs like pets. As puppies (cute little fur balls) they were allowed to roam freely until they turned six months of age. Abruptly they were then tied to a three-foot chain and were loosed only to pull the sleds. In the summer time they were fed only a fish a day – mere maintenance – because they were not working. This did not sweeten their dispositions and they were handled only by those in the family who would be driving them. Certain teams were considered meaner than others and could not be driven by anyone other than their owners.

Don and an Eskimo named Ralph, who had one of those more difficult teams, were out cutting ice one day when Ralph cut off part of two of his fingers and was unable to drive his team to the hospital. Don took over the handling of the team and drove them into town to the hospital. Don was greatly respected by the Eskimos, but this they couldn't believe. Everyone knew that only Ralph could handle this team!

I do not think huskies are innately vicious. They were simply hungry and largely ignored by their owners unless they were working. One of our students had a team that was approachable. He fed them well and worked with them daily. The local dentist (from Washington, I believe) had a team that was people-friendly. This was no doubt due to the fact that he spent time with his dogs and took good care of them. From this evidence I formed the opinion that huskies have the potential of being good companions to humans rather than just work dogs. It seems to depend on how they are treated.

The Alaskan husky is not a recognized breed. It is a descendent of Siberian huskies which were bred to be endurance sled pullers by the Chukchi Eskimos of northeastern Siberia. These were thought to have come to North America with the human migration at a time when a land bridge

ARCTIC CHALLENGE

connected Siberia and Alaska. Over the years they were cross bred with other dogs of various breeds selected for their sled pulling qualities. This led to the many different mixes of dogs that make up the Alaskan husky family.

Huskies range in color from white to very dark; from spotted to a solid color. Different groups of Eskimos developed dogs with slightly diverse characteristics. However, they all seem to have two characteristics - pointed ears that stand upright and tails that curl above their backs when they are alert and active. Huskies ready to run, with those plumes showing their eagerness, are a beautiful sight. When they sleep, their tails cover often their noses. They are all capable of sleeping out on the snow without harm. These are amazing dogs - intelligent and, according to some estimates, capable of traveling 40 miles a day pulling a load of 200 pounds each. The lead dog takes commands from the driver. The driver does not sit on the sled; he usually runs or walks along in the rear, riding a little every few minutes by standing on the rear of the sled. As you can see, drivers must also keep in shape.

Today dogs have been largely replaced by snowmobiles in Alaska. Dog sledding is now a sport, not a means of transportation. There were a few snowmobiles back in the 60's but they were known for breaking down or getting away from their owners. I remember flying from Noorvik to

Ruth Moline Eddy

Kotzebue and seeing an Eskimo running after his snowmobile on the vast snow-covered tundra. In the years that followed, the Eskimo managed to "tame" the snowmobile, or perhaps simply to understand the mechanics of it.

Getting back to the Alaskan husky: Any commentary on the qualities of the Alaskan husky would be lacking without the story of Balto, the wonder dog. In January of the year 1925 the town of Nome, Alaska, was experiencing an outbreak of diphtheria, a deadly, highly contagious disease at that time. Several Eskimo children had died and others had been diagnosed with the disease. Serum that could stop the impending epidemic was available only in Anchorage, a distance of nearly a thousand miles overland.

The method of transporting this serum would normally be by airplane but the two planes that were usually available had been disassembled and stored for the winter. A train could deliver the serum as far as Nenana – about a third of the way to Nome – but that left over 600 miles of treacherous terrain subject to frequent blizzards and temperatures 40 to 50 degrees below zero. In desperation it was decided that the only means of transportation that was feasible was by dog sled in a Pony-Express type relay. Twenty mushers and their dog teams were recruited for this effort.

ARCTIC CHALLENGE

It was estimated that the trip would take up to thirteen days.

The teams battled winds that were sometimes strong enough to knock over sleds and dogs. Yet, amazingly, the serum was delivered not in the expected thirteen but in just seven days. Gunnar Kaasen drove his team of huskies into Nome after enduring the brutal final 53 mile leg of the run in a blizzard with winds reaching 60 miles per hour and temperatures below -50 degrees Fahrenheit. Kaasen's part of the journey had not been planned to be the last leg; another team was to provide relief because of the severe weather conditions. But Kaasen became partially blinded by the blizzard and lost the trail. As a result, he missed the intended relief team, and he and his team had to try to make it all the way into Nome. The nearly blind sled master had to put his trust in Balto, his rookie lead dog, to find and follow the trail. Balto did his duty heroically and led the totally exhausted team into Nome after the 20 hour trip and delivered the serum. As a result, the epidemic was stopped. The press followed this story for days, and newspapers throughout the world carried Balto's picture on the front page.

The story of Balto has become a legend, with some accounts telling of his running all the way from the railroad handoff to the town of Nome – over 600 miles! I have tried to glean the facts and stick to them in telling this story – the facts are sensational enough. In 1995 a popular animated movie *Balto* was made, continuing his fame. A bronze statue of him stands in Central Park in New York City.

The sled dog race known as the Iditarod was first run in 1967 in commemoration of that famous accomplishment by these heroic men and their dogs. Now every year dozens of men and women train their dog teams specially for this highly-promoted, grueling memorial race from Anchorage to Nome on a designated route 1,200 miles in length.

ARCTIC CHALLENGE

Balto
**Dedicated to the indomitable spirit of the sled dogs
that relayed antitoxin 660 miles over treacherous
water, through Arctic blizzards, from Nenana to
the relief of stricken Nome in the winter of 1925
ENDURANCE   FIDELITY   INTELLIGENCE**

Balto's statue and plaque in New York City's Central Park

Ruth Moline Eddy

ARCTIC CHALLENGE

After the hunt

Ruth Moline Eddy

Tourists

One day while hanging clothes, what to my wondering eyes did appear – not Santa and his reindeer but a dog team pulling a sled on wheels. Riding on the sled were tourists; I discovered this was part of a Wein-Alaska Airlines promotion. They gave the tourists parkas to wear and drove them through the field near our house. I didn't mind that but I wanted to send them all back when they began peering into Eskimo homes.

In the summer many of the Eskimos close up their plywood or metal homes and move out on the coastal fields and beaches on Kotzebue Sound. The BIA doctors encouraged this because of the high rate of tuberculosis. It gave their permanent homes a chance to air out and lessen the contamination. The natives would bring most of their meager possessions, storing them in barrels and boxes outside their tents since they just wouldn't fit inside. The tourists pulled back the flaps of these summer homes and peered inside. It was rather obvious that someone was living in those tents. Anyway, tourists were a part of life in Kotzebue and some of them we found very enjoyable, especially since they could clue us in on what was happening in the lower forty-eight states. For information about the outside world, we had only ham radio and Nome's radio station (KICY) - few newspapers were available.

Tourists had mixed reactions to Kotzebue. Many were disappointed. Poverty is not pretty nor is lack of sanitation. Drying fish on racks everywhere does not exude an appealing fragrance. This was more like a trip to the remote regions of the Amazon than a trip to Paris or Venice. Here is what they did see: dogs and dog sleds, Eskimos - some in bright parkas and mukluks (boots) -, a sod igloo erected by the airlines, an Eskimo dance accompanied by skin drums and singers, boats, some of the native crafts such as ivory carving or bead working, and the so-called trading store where you could buy native products. Generally the groups came in mid-morning and left by late afternoon.

ARCTIC CHALLENGE

Kotzebue, early 1960's
Poverty is not pretty

Ruth Moline Eddy

ARCTIC CHALLENGE

Tundra and Mosquitoes

Most of the area surrounding us was the vast tundra. The tundra is an area of low, flat, treeless plains where the ground remains permanently frozen except for a few inches of the surface during the brief summer season. When the surface is not frozen it is a swampy place with humps of moss-covered and grassy earth called muskeg or tussocks which made it very difficult and tiring to walk on. It was impossible to set any kind of pace. We used to say that it would have been much easier to walk on the tundra if one leg were shorter than the other.

Tundra can also be found in the valleys of the Brooks Range, along with rock outcroppings. The tundra is a mysterious place – sometimes misty and seemingly uninhabited –, but it teems with life. For the numerous species of wildlife that spend at least part of their lives there, it is often a battleground with survival at stake. In the summer, viewing it from the air, it resembles a wide green highway covered with water-filled potholes. In the winter it is desolately beautiful – endless snow and ice with the spectacular reflections of the sunrises and, following within a short time, the sunsets functioning like colorwheels lighting up a Christmas display.

Robert Service, the English poet, expressed his love for Alaska in his poem, *The Spell of the Yukon*, a small portion of which follows:

> There's a land where the mountains are nameless,
> And the rivers all run God knows where;...
> There are hardships that nobody reckons;
> There are valleys unpeopled and still;
> here's a land – oh, it beckons and beckons,
> And I want to go back – and I will.

Robert Service had caught the thrill of viewing nature's vast expanses.

One thing Robert Service did not mention in his poem was the mosquito problem. During the short summer the mosquitoes live on the tundra in droves. Stories abound of both man and beast being driven insane by them. We ourselves had a serious encounter with them which I'll relate later.

Kotzebue was blessed with constant air movement due to the sea breezes which kept the mosquitoes at bay. The air was much quieter in Noorvik and Kiana and in June these insects were a plague. In villages like these, smoldering pine branches were the main repellant. Smoke near a home kept the mosquitoes at a distance and filled the air with a woodsy aroma. I am sure it was

ARCTIC CHALLENGE

also quite polluting and therefore probably not in the best interest of a population already struggling with tuberculosis.

I have been told that mosquitoes are important pollinators in the Arctic. So they seem to have their place in the environment. The mosquito problem had to be dealt with, however. The following is a quote from the Farmer's Almanac: "During the short summers of the Canadian arctic, swarms of mosquitoes are so intense that an unsuspecting man could be attacked some 9,000 times per minute, thereby losing half his blood in two hours."

We didn't experience anything that bad but we did get a taste of it. We took our boat, an open ten or twelve foot motorboat, from Noorvik to Kiana early one July and covered ourselves with netting – body, face and hands – but the moment we exposed any flesh the mosquitoes all but covered that area. Debbie did manage to get some facial bites and we had to take her to the first aid station in Kiana because her face was swelling. (Every village had a semi-trained Eskimo medical person who could confer with a doctor in Fairbanks by radio.) Sulfa was the medication designated and it took care of the swelling. We had intended to go farther upstream but decided it was too risky. There was nothing more we could have done to prepare us for these mosquito attacks.

Ruth Moline Eddy

Things would be better by August, we were told, but we decided to stick to the waters around Kotzebue and fly to inland areas. This was especially encouraged by the fact that Don and I had gotten the boat stuck on a sandbar in the Kobuk River northeast of Kiana. We had no idea when someone would come along in this part of the river to help us get loose. It could have been days. So it was up to us. We decided there was only one thing to do--try to dislodge the boat by standing in the water that covered the sandbar and PUSH. We did, and were finally able to loosen it, quickly climb aboard, and get out of there. A little risky (we could have been left standing there with the boat going on down the river) but it worked. Another one of those times where all you could do is trust. Fortunately, Debbie took it all in stride. What a child!

ARCTIC CHALLENGE

The tundra

Ruth Moline Eddy

ARCTIC CHALLENGE

School Begins

On Labor Day weekend we took a break and Harold Beck, the mission superintendent, flew us to Noorvik. Harold was a seasoned and trusted pilot and in a few weeks he would be picking up students within a 200 mile radius and bringing them in for school. Harold had a daughter just a little older than Debbie and they had a good time. I managed to get sick on the wild duck we ate there. Guess I couldn't expect to escape all of potential maladies present in this land.

When we got back to Kotzebue on Labor Day the students began arriving. Don and Harold took off again to pick up some students at Buckland and also Shungnak and Ambler, tiny villages upstream on the Kobuk River. All villages in this area are on rivers because that is the main means of transportation. In the winter the river became a highway for dog sleds. The planes also used it for landing after the pilots had exchanged their wheels for skis. In the summer many pilots replaced their skis with pontoons and seldom used wheels at all.

Ruth Moline Eddy

One summer the big event of the season was the submerging of a Weins Airlines float plane that tried to land at the waterfront with a punctured pontoon. It sank almost immediately but the pilot managed to get out in time. The drama of retrieving the plane lasted most of one day with spectators (myself included) glued to the scene. The huge crane that coaxed the plane out of the water resembled an oversized praying mantis intent on its prey. After the rescue the plane was shipped "stateside" for restoration.

Boats were the main means of transportation for the average resident of the Kobuk area, however. There were many kinds: wood, skin, fiberglass, covered, open – most of them powered by gasoline engines. One of the villages was built on both sides of the Kobuk River. In the summer time a visit with a friend or relative often meant a quick shuttle by boat across the river.

Tuesday morning, September 8, there were 16 eager students and we were officially in session even though the school building was not yet completed. The official name of the school was Friends High School because it was sponsored by the Friends (the Quakers). The church was called the Friends Church.

After registration we declared a work day. Students washed windows and cleaned up the main floor of the building. School began with classes in our house and the church. We did not

ARCTIC CHALLENGE

hold classes in the new building until September 28, twenty days after school officially began. At that, it was only two months to the day from the time the first forms were put in so that the foundation could be poured until the building was ready for classes. Except for the contractor and his assistant, we were all amateurs.

Students continued to come as late as September 17, and the last one came COD, that is, she came by commercial bush plane without the money to pay for her flight. We also got a young lady who had no place to live and so she stayed with us until her boyfriend came to Kotzebue a month later. Then she decided to get married instead. We discovered she was pregnant before she ever came to Kotzebue. I don't know if she didn't realize it or used the school as a way to bypass her parents and rejoin her boyfriend. He was from another village. Her parents (typically) wanted her to marry someone from their own village but did consent under the circumstances.

The weather was unusually mild and dry and we were able to work outdoors on the building until October 3. On the first Friday of school we had a get-acquainted party that set the tone for the year. The young people decided that these social kinds of events were going to be fun and so they were open to other activities. We formed a chorus that went to the hospital to sing for the patients; we had a drama club that gave plays for

Ruth Moline Eddy

the community; we developed a basketball team that played the local 7th and 8th graders as well as the men from the nearest military installation; we had game nights in the basement, and showed quite a few movies from the library in Fairbanks. We also started a Sunday school class and a singing group for the church.

A few students did not finish out the year. They just got too homesick for the outdoor life of hunting and fishing, especially if they found the schoolwork difficult. Adjustment to our routine was difficult for some of them because village life had no schedules and few rules.

Somewhere, somehow (probably through the BIA schoolteachers), Halloween became a part of Eskimo traditions. We had almost 100 trick-or-treaters visit our house. Unfortunately, more candy was not what these children needed. Because they already chewed bubble gum almost continuously, they had terrible teeth. We had become accustomed to seeing older women with stumps for front teeth, but these were the result of wear, not decay. When rounding the toes of the soles for mukluks, the women softened and shaped them by chewing them. (More recently they used pliers and similar tools.) The local government dentist had his hands full, especially since brushing one's teeth was not yet a fully accepted practice. At one time Eskimo bodies (with the exception of some of the women)

ARCTIC CHALLENGE

were found with nearly perfect teeth. Their diet originally contained no sweets or starches – just grasses, berries and meat; the more prosperous ones adding milk products from reindeer imported from Lapland. Incidentally, reindeer can be tamed; caribou cannot.

Speaking of caribou, that was our main source of meat and periodically Don and Harold the superintendent would fly out on the tundra and get a new supply. Sometimes the caribou were there by the thousands. Success was always guaranteed.

Besides the tooth problem another concern was one shared with us by the hospital personnel; that of body hygiene. Bathing was difficult – no running water, cold temperatures and virtually no privacy. There were often six to eight people in one or two tiny rooms. It was much easier to sleep in their daytime clothes. In addition, girls saved a lot of time by putting their hair up in bobby-pin curls and simply leaving them that way for several days. Washing clothes was also very difficult – melting snow produced little water and drying space was very scarce. We ourselves got a little tired of wet diapers hanging everywhere in our own house – no disposable diapers in those days.

By mid-October the temperatures were in the teens at night. In September we had watched the snow cover the tops of the mountains in the

Ruth Moline Eddy

Brooks Range. As the snow cover descended the mountains we knew it would soon arrive on the flat lands. As the temperature dropped the snow line came closer.

On October 20 Don had his first dog sled ride – out to the ice-cutting site. Into November most of the blocks could be hauled on the pick-up since the snow was not yet deep enough to stop the truck but it was important to keep going because any day could bring about a change. Hauling it in by dogsled would mean each load would be much smaller and the days continued to become shorter and colder.

In mid-November the public health nurse came to give shots and to demonstrate artificial respiration, as it was called. We decided that this was the week we would emphasize good grooming and cleanliness. We got really bold and told the girls they had to comb their hair before coming to school. (Many of the girls already did, but there had been a number of hold-outs.)

This was the beginning of a real turn-around. They liked what they saw and they really didn't overdo it. A few parents felt it took too much of their time (this was to be expected) but if we were to prepare their young people for the life many of them hoped to pursue in places like Fairbanks and Anchorage, they had to be presentable as well as educated. There were already too many young people in the Eskimo ghettos of those cities

ARCTIC CHALLENGE

locked into the very lowest level jobs. We wanted more for them than that. Besides, they had a new sense of confidence knowing that they looked nice. It helped them deal with the natural shyness that most of them had, a shyness that would be a handicap for them in making their way in any other than their own Eskimo culture. Incidentally, little Debbie was at this time exhibiting shy behavior, no doubt in imitation of the Eskimo children. More on that later.

I would like to add a bit more about the students. Those coming from the really small villages sometimes needed extra supervision. Since we had no dormitory facilities the first two years, they stayed with relatives or family friends. Perhaps in part because life was so fragile and many families had lost several children before the age of six (infanticide was no longer practiced by this time), they were reluctant to discipline their children. Though it grieved them when their children disobeyed they also felt it was something they had no control over. As a result, by the time they were in their early teens, young people, particularly in a larger town like Kotzebue often became intoxicated or ran the streets at night. We could not let this happen to those students entrusted to us from the villages.

Therefore, we had a certain amount of policing to do until we could show them a better way of

Ruth Moline Eddy

life. With the help of concerned people in town we were able to keep them out of any serious difficulties, but this kind of thing is stressful. Fortunately, the second year we had a teaching staff of five instead of three. Earl and Janice Perisho came from Oregon to teach in the school and also to direct the work of the church.

We never had any outright defiance from our students. If they were unhappy they would simply stay away or become withdrawn. On the other hand, if they were offended by something they were difficult to reason with. Usually it would take the intervention of another Eskimo to get things straightened out. We had several very level-headed students who were good at mediating. Fortunately, occasions requiring their services were rather few. After we were better acquainted with the adult Eskimos we found there were some of them whom we could call upon to talk with the students. They were very effective.

I might also mention another time-consuming development. I was three classes short of qualifying for an Alaska secondary certificate (I had only an elementary one) so I was given one year to complete the requirements. I did this by correspondence from the University of Nebraska.

One last note: On September 30 there was an encyclopedia salesman at my door! Was there any place on earth they did not go?

ARCTIC CHALLENGE

Thanksgiving and Christmas

In the meantime I had to begin a project of my own. It was the custom of the mission to give just about everyone in Kotzebue and the surrounding villages an article of clothing for Christmas. We had received thirty-seven barrels of clothing from churches in California via the annual freighter. My job was to sort these clothes into categories such as men's, women's, boys', girls', different children's sizes, etc. The Eskimo women would then come with their lists of people in their area and choose and wrap something for each one. They were remarkably accurate; usually they fit. This was also a wonderful way to get acquainted with the elderly Eskimo women as we worked together. We finished up on December 12, in time to get the boxes to the villages before Christmas.

In November the temperatures were mostly in the single digits down to zero. The big event of the month was the Thanksgiving dinner in the basement of the school. It was potluck featuring frozen fish, berries, caribou stew and muktuk (a kind of whipped whale blubber – eating it was something like eating lard). The caribou stew was wonderful; I often made it myself. The berries were tart but good in their own way; the frozen fish was not for me. And there was lots of homemade bread.

The really interesting thing was that the Eskimos came with small buckets and containers which they used like the "doggie bags" in restaurants. They would take a bowlful of stew, for instance, eat a third of it, and empty the rest into one of their pails. In fact, we could sometimes hear them instructing their children not to eat any more of a particular item but to put it in the pail instead. They had every intention of taking home at least as much as they had brought. How that works out mathematically, I am not sure. There must have been a number of people like us who brought considerably more than they consumed.

On December 1 the school report to the state was due. We had to report 45 incidents of students being tardy, so it was time for a few changes. We instituted some consequences for frequent tardiness. I believe that some of the more reliable students helped by making an effort to get some of the others there on time.

Preparations for Christmas were now in full swing. Home economics classes made decorations and cookies, eggnog, etc., and interested students practiced for a presentation of *A Christmas Carol*. On December 21, the shortest day of the year, we ran out of oil. I can't remember how that happened – delayed delivery perhaps, but we sent the students home. At this time the sun was just a slender red sliver that peeped above the horizon at 10:57 AM and slipped back at 12:40 PM, a total of 1 hour and 43 minutes of muted daylight.

The big event of Christmas was the church Christmas program followed by gift giving. The Eskimos brought most of their family gifts to the church to be given out in front of everyone. Packages were labeled and church officials called out the names. They then went forward to claim them. We took only one gift per family member since this was not our preferred way of giving. However, the Eskimos enjoyed seeing what each person got. This was an evening program and the whole event went from 6 PM to 11 PM.

A very special treat was in store for someone at the church gift-giving event. On a wire above the platform in front hung a pair of gorgeous mukluks – the knee-high ones that indicated that the wearer-to-be was considered to be a person of high rank. So everyone knew someone was to be honored that night and speculation ran high. The granting of the mukluks was the last event of the evening. It was Don whose name was called to receive the mukluks. He had absolutely no clue that he was to be the recipient, so he was rather dumbfounded but very pleased.

Ruth Moline Eddy

One year the event lasted until midnight with the temperatures outdoors at -36. With almost 700 people in attendance it was a warm place to be. For the next three days the temperature remained at -50 and the heating oil turned to slush. Out came the blow torches to warm the pipes enough to keep the oil moving. At that temperature the mail plane does not fly, so for three days we had no mail delivery.

The last really exciting event of the year routinely took place soon after Christmas. This was a series of dog races featuring local teams. There were men's races, women's races and youth races. Some of our students raced and did well. It was fun to watch.

The old year closed out with many people attending a New Year's service at the church. Others simply went out and got stone drunk. When Debbie was so small I did not attend the service, though I stayed up until the church bell stopped ringing. This was a huge bell that was rung with some vigorous pulls of a thick rope. This same bell was also the fire alarm for the town of Kotzebue. This bell is shown in the picture on page 29.

ARCTIC CHALLENGE

Winter in Kotzebue

Ruth Moline Eddy

ARCTIC CHALLENGE

The Inevitable Illnesses

We had been in Kotzebue for less than a week when Don was asked to perform a burial ceremony for a young boy who died of one of the white man's diseases – measles. This disease was often fatal as the Eskimo had little resistance it.

At Eskimo funerals there was no longer the wailing, shrieking or chanting that had once been the norm. The men of the church would make a suitably-sized plywood coffin (measurements would be taken); the box would usually be covered with a flowered oilcloth, the body placed inside and artificial flowers placed on top. The ceremony would be brief with a message of comfort and often included an admonition to take preparation for eternity seriously. Mourners would attend in an orderly manner, often weeping quietly but definitely controlled. I did see one exception to that. The only son of an Eskimo man working in Fairbanks died of complications from measles. The man flew home for the funeral but then felt he could not look at his dead son. He didn't want to see him that way. Apparently the elderly women had some ideas about the importance of closure. Three or four of them took hold of him bodily and marched him down the center aisle of the church to take that one last look, the man resisting the entire way.

Somehow our children, Debbie and Jerry, did not get either measles or chicken pox while these diseases were taking their toll in the village during the years we were there. (Debbie's brother Jerry was born about two years after our arrival in Kotzebue – more on that later.) However, within a couple of months after our arrival back in Michigan they picked up both diseases. Now, since the development of immunizations for these diseases, neither measles nor chicken pox is a threat to the Eskimos, just as it is not a threat to other children in the western world.

We were part of an interesting study about midway through our four years there. The Eskimos were being tested for the amount of radiation in their body tissues which was then compared to what they found in non-natives. We tested between 60 and 80 (I don't recall what the measure was called) and the Eskimos tested over 300. Fallout from nuclear testing in Siberia was the cause of the elevated counts in Eskimos. Tundra grass absorbed the radiation, caribou ate the grass and the Eskimos ate the caribou. We did, too, but not for a lifetime like they did. Apparently the most remote areas of the world

ARCTIC CHALLENGE

are hardly free of even the worst kinds of contamination.

Due to the extremely unsanitary conditions, the Arctic held the threat of diseases such as typhoid, dysentery, tuberculosis and hepatitis. Little Jerry suffered from dysentery and Don got hepatitis, but we got yearly shots for typhoid and regular checks for exposure to tuberculosis and escaped those two maladies.

Towards the end of April 1960 there began a period of several weeks where I was sick a good share of the time – stomach, throat, a little fever. About the time I was better, Don got sick and he started to turn yellow! Infectious hepatitis, Dr. Frasier said. Into the hospital he went. I, and also an Eskimo student who was staying with us, had gamma globulin injections and did not get it.

The Eskimos were so good to Don and looked out for him during his recovery from hepatitis. With permission from the doctor they took him along on some seal hunts. All he had to do was sit in the boat in the somewhat warm June sun and watch. He enjoyed this to the fullest and made a fine recovery.

I have previously mentioned Don's polio and his remarkable recovery, so yes, we had some concerns about how he would fare under these severe Arctic conditions. I do believe, however, that had the Arctic cost him his life he would have died happy; he seemed to be happiest when he was out hunting or fishing with the natives. He not only enjoyed this part of Arctic life, he enjoyed teaching, and appreciated the fact that his wife was willing to put up with some inconveniences to make it all possible.

As I mentioned, little Jerry got dysentery and it was hard when I could feed him only water with a bit of salt and sugar in it for several days at a time but he was a wonderful child and with a little extra attention and diversion he got through those episodes all right.

In my journal the entry "Debbie sick" occurred a number of times but probably not too much more often than for a child her age in more temperate climates. We were about two blocks from a hospital and had access to a doctor 24 hours a day.

A few years before going to Alaska I had taught school in what would be called a slum area – an experience that proved to be a unique preparation for what lay ahead. My adventures as a teacher in "shantytown" in Wichita, Kansas, were far more dangerous and stressful than anything I would experience in the Arctic. In shantytown people destroyed things so that they could claim new ones; burned down their shacks to get insurance money. The kids put sand in people's gas tanks and stopped up their chimneys, and no one from outside the area went there after dark – not even the police if they could avoid it. In fact, the county education leadership refused (or was not able) to staff the school, but a veteran male teacher with a vision of what Christian training could do and a real love for children agreed to take it over and try to turn it around. It was a three-year agreement.

I joined the staff in the third year and missed some of the worst of it – the student behavior had improved to the point where it was controllable. This was all the more impressive in light of the fact that in general the neighborhood was as tough as ever. I was elated the day the other teachers and I lost our jobs because the school was now safe enough for any qualified teacher and the county took it back. I could have been rehired but I felt I had done what I could and I wanted to go back to college for a degree in social work, which I did.

Yes, there was danger in Alaska but after my experiences in Wichita I was able to keep these risks in perspective. As I have mentioned, there was the threat of disease from extremely unsanitary conditions. Then there were the occasional drunken Eskimos but at least they weren't driving cars and there were very few snowmobiles back then. Besides, they were more likely to pass out than to become violent. I was often asked how I could take a young child to such a severe, forsaken place, and my reply was that she was in less danger than she would have been crossing a busy city street or riding in a car on one of our highways stateside. Statistically she was safer, I'm sure. In fact, one of the missionaries who safely raised a daughter in Noorvik later lost her when she was killed by a car in California while she was out jogging. Little Debbie's encounter with the dogs had taught her to keep her distance from them and she quickly learned to recognize other dangers as well, as all children do.

We flew into the "bush" occasionally, without incident. Flying, too, was in Don's blood and after we returned to Michigan he earned his pilot's license and flew all over the state and back and forth to Chicago. Again, statistically, he was in more danger here than he was when flying with veteran pilot Harold Beck in the uncrowded skies over Alaska.

We really had little to fear in a community where people shared what they had; stealing was almost unknown, and if there was danger other than that which I've mentioned, it was usually an Eskimo putting his own life and limb at risk out of sheer frustration or lack of rational thinking.

ARCTIC CHALLENGE

The Eskimo Language

The Eskimo language was not a written language until the 1940's when a German Bible translator by the name of Wilford Zibell produced the book of Mark. I have one of the original copies and it states "St. Mark in Eskimo: Barrow" (Barrow indicates the dialect, for there were many). We knew Wilford personally as he would come to Kotzebue for a few weeks at a time for the purpose of researching the language. There are sounds in Eskimo that do not have a parallel in the English language and so there are a few rather strange-looking letters. In addition, their words are often very long; sometimes they are as long as our entire alphabet. One such word is "talimakipiallaaguvallinazut" (the n looks like it has a j hooked on to it and other letters have diacritical marks such as dots and wavy lines above or below them to indicate a variation in the pronunciation). We have the same kind of thing in the German language. I learned a few often used phrases such as, "Tavza ilaan ukalautinagai" for "And he said". The preponderance of u's, i's, and k's is evident in this short five word sentence from Zibell's translation: "Kupilgunic tukulaicut sulii ignik kamilaicuk".

Without a written language the Eskimos were limited in learning about things they had never seen or in expressing ideas that were new. They had no alphabet or phonetic symbols as we do, but they could communicate with a kind of picture writing. Because of our alphabet we can express just about anything on paper.

Still, in their society the lack of a written language was not as great a handicap as it would be in ours since they were an isolated people with only basic needs. They were intelligent and resourceful, however. They had to be in order to survive; those who weren't died.

So, at first my feelings about the value of putting the Eskimo languages in a phonetic form were mixed. It was an incredible task and by the time we came upon the scene it seemed of limited use since many Eskimos were able to order from a Sears catalog with its combination of words and pictures. Most of their children were learning English in the BIA elementary schools and could help their parents and grandparents.

On the other hand, in spite of the trend toward phasing out the Eskimo language in the 60's, it is spoken in the streets and in public gatherings even today. Apparently the efforts of the translators were instrumental in preserving the language.

ARCTIC CHALLENGE

You will have observed that I refer to Eskimos by names common in English. That is because the missionaries gave them all English names, and I think you can see why. They simply could neither pronounce nor remember those lengthy monikers. The Eskimos in turn, named our children. Debbie was Kalliuk, the pretty one, and Jerry was Kinnuksiruk, the one with the wide mouth. The Eskimos were named for some event or some physical characteristic.

I later discovered that Jerry was named after Mark Jones who was "the one with the wide mouth" and was the patriarch of the native church. So it was quite an honor that the Eskimos had chosen that name for him. Mark Jones was a very intelligent and progressive Eskimo – with an almost forbidding countenance, but he was as compassionate a person as you'll ever find. He was one of those who could read both the translated Eskimo and the English.

Ruth Moline Eddy

ARCTIC CHALLENGE

Eskimo children dressed for winter

Ruth Moline Eddy

ARCTIC CHALLENGE

Teaching the Children

When the Eskimos chose the path of Christianity over the shaman's system of ritual and taboo, the Ten Commandments became their guide. Besides wanting an education for their children, the parents had another reason for requesting the establishment of the high school. They had hopes that the Biblical values they had learned from the missionaries would be instilled in their young people. As I have said, the parents were not good disciplinarians. It was becoming more and more difficult for the parents to keep outside influences from "corrupting" the children. Not that there weren't enough of those influences already in some of the larger villages. So the goals of the Friends mission and the needs and desires of the Eskimo parents coincided in making it our responsibility to establish a quality school as well as to encourage the youth in the ways of Christianity.

Teaching bilingual young people from such a remote area required a somewhat altered approach at times. We used standard texts purchased from the large publishing companies most schools utilize. However, many of the experiences alluded to in those texts had never been a part of the lives of our students. I remember walking by one of the classrooms and hearing one of the teachers describe traveling by train, sound effects and all. At first I laughed because it sounded like story time for a three year old. However, I'm sure most three year olds in the "lower 48" had experienced more of the subject matter of the textbooks than had our teenagers. In time we surmounted a good deal of the deficiency through educational films from the University of Alaska at Fairbanks. In some cases there were also some adjustments to the reading level of the books we were using. Sometimes we read together in class and when it was needed all of the teachers made themselves available for tutoring. This was usually done after school or on Saturdays.

Our students' vocabulary was a bit limited at first, but they learned not only from us but from each other, and except for a bit of an accent, they progressed rapidly. We knew exposure to some of the things they studied would provide impetus to learning so we had people in from the University to talk to the students whenever possible. We had mineralogists, people from health and human services – any knowledgeable person that we could coerce into meeting with our students when they came to town. From our

ARCTIC CHALLENGE

own community we had professionals such as doctors and dentists. Field trips took us behind the scenes at the post office, the small branch office bank, the airport and the DEW line installation. The airport arranged to have a full-sized replica of a space capsule bought in.

Our basketball team flew to the "city" of Nome for a game. Friends High did not win the game but they gave it their best. They had beaten the National Guardsmen one or twice; that was enough to keep them inspired. I got a surprise upon Don's return from Nome. He brought a package of genuine BEEF hamburger back with him – "the wonderful taste of home" – the only time we had it in our four years in Alaska.

Almost without exception our high school students had very wholesome boy-girl relationships. In most ways the students were like students anywhere. Alice was bright and athletic, and very pretty (She transferred to Anchorage in her junior year and did just as well there). Norm was subject to seizures and had a hard time keeping up but he didn't quit. Herman was shorter than most of the girls and got revenge by giving them a hard time. They were always complaining about him. Eventually they learned to ignore him and he in turn began to treat them like bona fide human beings. I suspect that in time he married one of them. Susie adored Mike and couldn't keep her eyes or mind off him.

Ruth Moline Eddy

Jane was bigger and tougher then most of the boys and constantly challenged them to arm wrestling matches. Paul was moody and tended to make curt replies. Usually no one was at all concerned about it; he had always been that way. He did improve somewhat. Glen was shy and preferred his own company but was never rude about it. Naturally we also had a few giggly girls. A well-rounded student body was the way I looked at it. Who would have it otherwise?

From the Friends High News (the student newspaper) comes this short article:

> I WONDER WHO – Always sits between the two stoves in church?
> Often gives silly answers because he's not listening to the questions?
> Might have won the dog race if his dogs hadn't gone home?
> Is considered the strongest girl in school? (our arm wrestler)
> Cackles like a hen laying an egg?
> Fell off the truck when the boys were hauling ice?

All of this is so typical of high school though the subject matter is a bit different. We encouraged formal debates in order to increase their ability to speak up and verbally defend themselves. A few of the topics they chose for debating were:

ARCTIC CHALLENGE

> Hunting polar bear by plane should be outlawed.
> A fish cannery should be established in Kotzebue.
> The curfew for young children who run around after midnight in the summer should be abolished.

One of the junior boys wrote out this well-stated argument for that last topic prior to presenting it:

> Some laws seem to do more harm than good as in this case. In this town the youngsters have a habit of playing out until the wee hours of the morning during the summer months. Well, I don't blame them. When the midnight sun is shining, which is very beautiful, the air is cool and refreshing and it's very hard to try to sleep in a gloomy, colorless house. When a curfew law was passed, the results were sad. It was hard for the kids to break this habit but the kids finally learned to obey that law very well. Now it seems as if their energy is gone. I don't see them playing real hard and having fun at some sport. Some of the most athletic kids now sit around a juke box and snap their fingers for exercise. I would rather see the kids lose a little of their sleep and toughen their bodies. I think a strong body and mind go together in living successfully in this world. Then, too, it is the parent's duty to see that his child is home if he wants him to go to bed at a certain hour.

This law did not stay in effect very long and possibly this young man's ability with words had some influence. Another male student expressed his longings in a titleless poem:

> I should like to rise and go
> Where the apples, oranges and fruits grow.
> Where it's warm and lively,
> Where I could see many things, laugh, and have fun,
> And forget everything I leave behind--
> And go on to see a new world.

Ironically, to the best of my knowledge, this young man was one who never left the Arctic. Many of our students were a year or two behind in their language skills when they began high school, but progress was often spectacular for those who really wanted to learn. An honor roll provided some incentive also.

Sunday mornings presented some additonal teaching opportunities. During the lengthy Eskimo services, a number of the Eskimo women and I held a children's church in the basement of the school. We tried to alternate activity with listening time and many children attended – on some occasions as many as eighty. They really loved singing *Jesus Loves Me* in English, Spanish and Eskimo. When I arrived on the scene, I taught it to them in German. What an achievement they considered this to be – four languages! And what fun to teach these delightful, wiggly, shy but eager children!

ARCTIC CHALLENGE

Our First School Year Ends

Almost before we were ready for it, it was Good Friday and just a bit below zero. We had promised the ninth graders a picnic on the hills near the lagoon so off we went. The hot dogs we roasted over a fire had to be popped into our mouths quickly so they wouldn't refreeze. We drank hot tea rather quickly also. I had my first dog sled ride that day.

On Sunday there was a sunrise service at 4 AM – that's when the sun rose. A week later the temperature reached 48 degrees. The next day it fell to -22 overnight.

As you might expect, even though we held classes and had all the necessary equipment, the school still needed many finishing touches like paint, floor coverings, drapes and library shelves. We continued to work on these throughout the year. We charged a small tuition fee which students could work off if they could not afford even that small fee. The work afforded a fine opportunity for earning tuition credit and was helpful to both the students and to us. The finishing touches on the apartment would wait until the summer.

Ruth Moline Eddy

The school year had ended with an inspiring awards assembly but we had one final concern. The dozen or so students from the entire Kobuk region who had been chosen to attend the Eskimo high school in Mt. Edgecumbe were due to arrive in Kotzebue in another two days (most would then go on to their home villages). Our question was: how will Friends High School stack up and how will our students compare to these elite? How will they get along? When these Mt. Edgecumbe students left Kotzebue for school in August our school had been little more than a framework. None of us knew what the facilities at Mt. Edgecumbe were like and we were aware that our scholastic standards might have been a bit lower since we were accepting anyone with passing grades. We wondered how the two groups would get along. We did not want our students to be embarrassed by possible comparisons.

It was decided that we would meet this challenge aggressively, so Ron Woodward, our young, handsome male teacher threw a welcome-home party for the returning students. It proved to be a good move. The next day (Sunday) nine of them showed up in our Sunday School class, perhaps out of curiosity. A teen class was a new thing. Up to this time teens could only sit in the adult classes, taught mostly in Eskimo, which was not their preference. Since our students were now as well-dressed and groomed as the visitors were, and for the most part conducted themselves with some maturity (there will always be at least one joker), the two groups blended well. In fact, a couple of them decided to remain in Kotzebue for schooling. One of them was a member of the first graduating class.

It was the season for wearing sun glasses. Earlier Eskimos had improvised a version of sun glasses with a thin layer of caribou hoof with a slit in it. Protection for the eyes was essential because the bright sunshine on the snow caused snow blindness, usually temporary, but still very real while it lasted. This was the time of year that many of the Eskimos were very dark – they were suntanned on face and hands.

In mid-June Don was well on the way to recovery from hepatitis and felt well enough to do the wiring in the apartment. On July 2 a work crew of eight teenage boys came from California to help finish the building project and do some sightseeing. They attended the 4th of July festivities in Kotzebue. The big event was the blanket toss. In this activity a number of people form a circle around a walrus-hide blanket which had handholds cut around the edges. They use this crude but effective trampoline to toss a person as high as they can for as long as the participant can remain upright. And to what heights they were tossed – absolutely incredible!

Ruth Moline Eddy

This was a competition with loudspeakers announcing and commenting on each participant. There were Eskimo drummers - using skins on a round willow hoop that they beat with sticks on the open underside. There were also singers and dancers.

The blanket toss originated as a means of looking for whales, walrus, seals or other game off in the distance by flinging an observer high into the air. It is very popular in the Arctic and virtually all Eskimo festivals include this activity.

The work crew of teenage boys from California was also here for part of the yearly Quarterly Meeting so they had some unique experiences, including flights to some of the villages. The boys were a real help with strenuous tasks that required lifting, digging and climbing. Debbie, now almost two years old, really enjoyed the boys. She seldom lacked attention. The Eskimo people, including the students, loved her and were fascinated by her deep blue eyes.

And now it was arrival time for the annual freighter from Seattle. The California work team left just before some of our goods began arriving at the dock from the freighter out at sea and that left us short-handed. Besides our groceries and house wares; school supplies, typewriters, clothes for the Eskimos, boxes of flooring tiles and a table saw for shop class had to be hauled to the school

ARCTIC CHALLENGE

The Blanket Toss

Ruth Moline Eddy

ARCTIC CHALLENGE

and put in place. We also still had many hours of work left on our apartment.

Suddenly our Kotzebue students were there – painting, laying tiles, putting in fuel lines (our stove and oven used oil as fuel, as did the furnace). They also did most of the carrying of boxes from the truck into our apartment and into the "big house" where the Eckels, a new teaching couple, would now be living. The Eckels, Quakers from California, were not novices; they were veteran village BIA teachers who went back to the "lower 48" but missed Arctic teaching enough to return. The following year, another couple, Earl and Janice Perisho, teachers from Oregon, would occupy that house. They would stay for quite a few years.

Now Don and Harold had to go hunting again to restock our meat supply (moose this time) so the students and I were left to do the moving of our supplies. We completed the work on the very day the Eckels arrived, perhaps an hour or two before their plane landed. Sadly, some years later one of the Eckels' sons was to lose his life in a plane crash over the Arctic.

Nine days later our second year of school began. We had a small surprise before that, however. On the Sunday before Labor Day the assistant to the State Educational Director came to visit our school. The state was becoming interested in what was going on here.

Ruth Moline Eddy

Our Second School Year Begins

Winter came earlier in 1960. By mid-September the Brooks Range was completely snow-covered and we had had some snow ourselves. We had some rocky starts in the school. Two of our students got pneumonia and spent about a week in the hospital. A brother and sister decided they couldn't handle it and went home. Two girls disappeared from the homes of relatives they were staying with and it took us nearly a week to find them and take them home. Coming to school was just a ruse to get out of their tiny village. They simply moved about to people's homes and by the time we discovered where they were they had moved on to someone else's. What stories they told in order to be sheltered like that we'll never know.

Fortunately things settled down after that; the sick recovered and we had a good year. One of the things we found ourselves having to do was to be open to allowing students to live with us in our home, at least on a temporary basis. We couldn't just let the students go home if things went wrong where they were staying. The two we had with us finally left for other arrangements, and then Mary came. Her mother was an alcoholic who periodically kicked her out of the home. Things got so bad that Mary could not really concentrate on her studies and we had her come to the relative quiet of our home. She was good with Debbie and willing to help me when needed. We also had several boys stay with us off and on, and finally we had the local elementary school principal's son, who was also one of our students. His dad had to go stateside for a few months and he didn't want to have his son switch schools twice in one year.

I did not manage to complete all of the work of my correspondence course that first spring. I was unable to finish the last course because I did not have access to many of the books I needed as reference in order to complete my work. The nearest library for that was in Fairbanks, a plane flight away. So I was stalled, but the way out of that dilemma presented itself quite unexpectedly, as I'll explain later.

Coming to school regularly and on time was a start on developing a work ethic. Being responsible for completing homework and long-term projects was another step. An example of the success of this program was the record of one of the two first graduates of the school – perfect attendance for all four years! Our school had been established for only three years at that time but he had previously attended the temporary school set up by the earlier missionaries.

Juniors and seniors, most of whom had developed a sense of responsibility in the process of getting that far in their schooling, were given the opportunity to experience the world of work locally. One of our goals was to teach them how to work with and for the "white folks" so we arranged a program with the merchants, the shipping companies, the hospital, etc. for some practical work experience. To instill a work ethnic was a bigger job than we bargained for, but it was, for the most part, accomplished through this program.

Those who accepted these students into their program knew that they were young and very inexperienced. They didn't get paid at first; it was up to the employer to decide if and when they would. We kept track of how things were going, and sometimes we had to encourage both students and their overseers to be patient.

A few of these young workers experienced considerable job stress and the companies which had accepted them found they worked too slowly to be of much benefit to them. Occasionally a student would become discouraged and want to give up. We would then beg for patience from both employer and student. To the companies' credit they usually were persuaded to provide some latitude. It was always a morale booster when a student improved to the point of being able to finish out his or her designated tenure.

We also had some who proved to be really proficient workers – especially one of the boys who worked in the general store. He learned quickly and was very conscientious. And Steve, the boy who lived with us, was a whiz. He became a prized worker. A little aside on Steve: When he first came to enroll, he was so short and thin that I took him to be someone's little brother. He was quick to inform me that he had finished the 8th grade. When Steve graduated four years later he was the tallest boy in the school. I have often wondered if the change in diet (he ate with us for well over a year) had anything to do with his growth spurt. Steve went on to college in Oregon and then joined the Air Force. After that we lost track of him.

All in all the heads of the businesses and institutions in the community were very understanding. They knew that some of these young folks would not succeed but they were willing to give them an opportunity to try their wings and give them a taste of what the working world was like.

Some of the business people also helped make it possible for Kotzebue to have a very nice little library – the Bullocks of the shipping company, the Rotmans of the general store, and the German couple, the Eckhardts who ran the touristy trade post, to name a few. Mrs. Eckhardt's husband died while we were there and we thought she'd leave the area but she didn't. She always called Don "the professor" and would give him some of her trinkets every time he came in. He spaced his visits eventually because he was afraid she'd go bankrupt.

Another person who was helpful was Jim Hayes. He married an Eskimo lady, then built a basement house with a room on top to raise chickens. We really enjoyed those fresh eggs. He also joined us in our efforts to keep alcohol away from the Eskimo youth.

Harmon Williams, a very tall black man from Philadelphia was also helpful. He was fascinated by the ice cutting and would come out to lend his assistance. Harmon was one of those who left almost as suddenly as he came. No one knew why Harmon was in Kotzebue or why he left, but then no one knew what brought other people from the "outside" to this land, and seldom did anyone ask. As one of the pioneers from the outside said, "Most of them are running away from someone or something so we don't ask questions."

ARCTIC CHALLENGE

A Trip to the Lower States and a New Baby

On April 27, 1961, Debbie and I flew to Chicago, leaving Don in Alaska. The previous October I had learned that I was pregnant. I would not be permitted to have the baby at the BIA hospital because I was not Eskimo or Indian. It was decided that I would go to Elgin, Illinois, where Don's parents lived. While there I would have access to the books I needed to complete my school work.

Five days before my departure about forty-five Eskimo ladies had a shower for me. They made all kinds of baby clothing and boots plus trinkets for me. I still have most of these. The most amazing part was a little speech by Lisa Roberts who was probably the most prominent elderly Eskimo lady in that entire region. With tears running down her cheeks she said to me personally and to the group as a whole, "You cannot know what this occasion means. You are being honored even though we do not know if this child is going to be a girl or a boy. Such a thing could not have happened a few years ago.

Ruth Moline Eddy

When my twin sister and I were born we were left on the ice to die. The missionaries rescued us." Her further testimony would be that neither did she any longer fear the evil spirits. Lisa had converted to Christianity like so many others and her new faith had replaced fear with peace.

During the shower, while eating the refreshments, I noticed several women looking at me and laughing but I chose to ignore it. Finally one of them asked me if I knew what I was eating. Looking at the finely chopped greens on my plate, I replied, "Tundra greens". Now laughing uncontrollably she replied, "From a caribou's stomach!" She expected a look of horror which she didn't get. Compared to the fish eyeball soup and the rancid seal oil they ingested, this was apple pie. I regret that I cannot remember the details of the Eskimo games they played that night. They were active games with lots of movement and lots of silliness but it was wholesome and refreshing. They knew how to have fun.

I had a good month in Elgin before Jerry was born and I got most of my schoolwork done. Jerry was born June 8, 1961, and a front page article in the local newspaper was headlined *Baby Escapes Being Born in an Igloo*. What a riot! I did take my books along to the hospital in case I would be detained there any length of time. I completed the library portion of the assignment about a week later. We then flew to Quakertown in Bucks County, Pennsylvania to visit with my parents, my siblings and their spouses, Esther and Paul, Dina and Henry. The three of us – Debbie, Jerry and I – were back in Kotzebue on July 10, two and a half months after leaving, and almost exactly two years from the date of my first arrival.

Ruth Moline Eddy

Summertime and a Visit from the U-2

Back to the busy life! It was Quarterly Meeting time again and that meant hundreds of Eskimos in town for that event. It was also tourist season and there were visitors for us to entertain. Besides that, the local people came to see the new baby. Jerry was a very alert and responsive baby – and he, like Debbie, had big blue eyes. The Eskimos commented on how interesting it must be to speculate on what color eyes and hair a child would have. They could be certain of black hair and brown eyes.

This was salmon time and we processed about 200 pounds. Arctic salmon has to be one of the tastiest foods on the planet. We usually ate it several times a week. Eskimo men caught the salmon in nets for their own personal use and there were also commercially owned salmon ships out in the sea. The commercial fishermen not only caught the salmon but canned it right on the ship. The more enterprising Eskimos worked on those ships during the summer and were paid relatively well. Unfortunately, many of them spent most of their earnings before they ever

ARCTIC CHALLENGE

returned to their homes. The Eskimos and the mission personnel also caught trout, whitefish, bass and grayling. The most interesting was a native fish called a shee fish, very large and not too plentiful. It was considered a delicacy and we only had it a few times. It was a specialty on the menu of the local hotel, along with sourdough pancakes.

During this month of August we awaited the arrival of an additional teacher, Glenna Nickell. She had been a teacher to the children of the scientists at the Mt. Palomar observatory in California but was ready to try something new. The upstairs of the big house was being converted into a dormitory for girls and she would be in charge. The renovations, of course, would be made by our own personnel, who also would be occupied by freight coming in by the truckload (the annual ship had arrived). Some duck hunting and fishing had to be squeezed in before the really cold weather set in but by Labor Day we were ready as a result of putting in some rather long hours of work. Then four days of heavy rain delayed flying in the students. We also had a terrible wind storm that wrecked boats and badly damaged some roofs. At the airport winds were clocked at 115 miles per hour, but thankfully, temperatures were still above freezing.

When the skies cleared, the flying in of the students resumed. On one flight our mission

Ruth Moline Eddy

pilot met a Soviet plane flying below the radar in the mountain passes of the Brooks Range. They passed so closely that he could see the pilot's face. About this time military observers were also reporting nuclear tests in Eastern Siberia – nine in one week.

A little over a year later during the Cuban missile crisis the Kotzebue airport was the landing site for the U-2 that had been shot at over Siberia. It was escorted by four very loud F-105 fighters. The noise was enough to get us all out of our homes and into the streets to see what was going on. Our mission plane was en route back to Kotzebue but had to turn back as all flights were banned while the U-2 was being repaired and fueled. It took off ten hours later. It appeared to go almost straight up and was gone in no time.

That autumn at about the time of freeze-up, we wondered briefly if a Soviet invasion really had begun. We heard a plane nearby and then saw a group of paratroopers descend in the area of the lagoon. After reaching the ground they picked themselves up and hiked the mile or so to the airport where the plane had landed. Although we never did find out what that was all about, we concluded that it was a U.S. military training maneuver. Somehow it was not considered necessary or advisable to inform the citizenry as to the purpose of this drop.

ARCTIC CHALLENGE

This proximity to the Soviet boundaries was a problem for the Eskimos as well. In the Bering Strait, between Alaska and Siberia, Little Diomede Island was part of Alaska, but the Soviets owned Big Diomede Island just a very few miles away. The International Date Line runs between them so there is always a day's time difference between them. Eskimos living on Little Diomede were related to those on Big Diomede but dared not cross the invisible line dividing the waters. It did happen a few times and the trespassing Alaskan Eskimos were taken captive. I believe that eventually all were returned but I am not sure. Most, if not all, of the trespassing was accidental and occurred in connection with their normal hunting of whales, seals, walrus, etc. The Diomede Eskimos were talented ivory carvers and engravers, the ivory coming from walrus tusks.

Ruth Moline Eddy

Dishonesty Knows No Racial Barriers

The Eskimos are quite trusting – almost childlike. An example: A magazine salesman came to Kotzebue with the usual high pressure pitch. In this case it was "You pay only the postage; the magazines are free". The word *free* is a magic word to an Eskimo. So, in spite of the fact that most of the older Eskimos could barely speak English let alone read it, they signed contracts for magazines they knew nothing or very little about, sometimes very likely with an X for a signature. I found out about it when one of the ladies showed me her contract. When I told her what the contract said and how much money she would have to pay out, she was, of course, very upset. At that point I contacted the company and very emphatically informed them of how one of their representatives had taken advantage of an unsuspecting people. To their credit, they gave me a certain number of days in which to collect any contracts the people were displeased with and return them to the company for cancellation.

ARCTIC CHALLENGE

The Eskimos are intelligent and do learn, sometimes very quickly. In the 60's they had a scheme they worked by which they got aid to dependent children (the old ADC). If they became the main source for a child's welfare, even if the child was not their own, they could receive payments. So, they traded children. "You take three of mine and I'll take three of yours and we'll both get paid". I don't know if this kind of thing still works or not. Another deal they worked was to put in just enough hours on the floating fish canneries in the summer to be eligible for unemployment benefits. Then they would quit or just not return. This may be something they are no longer able to do, I really don't know. I do know they have discovered the dole.

I realize that some of what the Eskimos did for income wasn't legal but there were no agencies or policing structures locally and no one ever came to check on anything. There was a justice of the peace but he was an eccentric, very benign elderly bachelor who was kind of a hermit and seldom seen outside his home except for his turn at the community library – a responsibility he and I shared. He was available when needed for notarizing papers, etc.

Ruth Moline Eddy

Our Third Year

During our third year Don was asked to be on the town council. This meant quite a few meetings and I was on the library council and also attended a number of meetings. The town "fathers", mostly Eskimo, were fighting an attempt to do away with laws that forbade the importing of liquor. That is not to say that Kotzebue was totally "dry", but at least alcohol was not sold openly. There was a certain amount that found its way into the hands of those who wanted it badly enough. All too often frozen bodies were found – people who drank and then got lost or who went into a stupor and never woke up again.

Near the close of our fourth year the importing of liquor was made legal and Kotzebue became "free-flowing". This multiplied the community's social problems and increased the number of unscrupulous profiteers. The one plus I see in this situation was that people stopped drinking after-shave and other substances with alcohol content. Hopefully they didn't drink this stuff straight but considering the black tar they drank (thick coffee)

ARCTIC CHALLENGE

perhaps they were able to do that too. They'd come to our house and sit for hours drinking coffee and remaining wide awake enough to stay until very late. One could not suggest they leave – that would have been the grossest violation of hospitality possible.

Back to our third year: At the beginning of the school year we finally had a girls' dormitory. That year three houses burned. Mary's house burned and the old abandoned hospital building also burned. No one was injured but that old wooden building made a spectacular fire. Fortunately the new hospital was already in place. There was no fire-fighting equipment and if there had been, it would have been useless during the winter months when the temperatures are so low and the water frozen. That was the year Ralph cut off part of two fingers while sawing ice blocks and Don put him on his dog sled and drove the dog sled and him to the hospital. That year also a young Eskimo man took his own life, followed by another a few weeks later. In addition, a number of children died that year, most of them of complications from measles.

On the lighter side, our Siamese cat had kittens. It was intriguing to watch these tiny little bodies develop and their all-white fur become tinged with dark marking on the nose, ears, and tail. It was people from the lower 48 who brought cats to the Arctic. They gave us ours. The Eskimo people had too many dogs and they (the dogs) would usually kill a cat if they could get close enough to catch it.

Once again it was Christmas. We had the same silver-colored aluminum tree we had used on previous Christmases but it looked good to us. The following Christmas was an exception to the aluminum Christmas tree tradition. Don and another local pilot went out to hunt, supposedly. They came back with real live Christmas trees. What a treat in a treeless environment! In addition we had a string of lights around our living room window.

The 2003 Alaska Almanac contains an article about the "Kotzebue National Forest". Of course the tundra is treeless but there was an actual single, three foot white spruce growing on the tundra outside of Kotzebue. It was there some twenty years, supposedly planted by homesick personnel from the Air Force installation outside of town. Someone put up a sign identifying it as the "Kotzebue National Forest". Maliciously, someone cut it down. This parallels what happened to us at the first house we lived in. Two small spruce trees grew beside the house and there was also a plastic-covered greenhouse in which we grew radishes, lettuce, and carrots one summer. This was possible because of the long daylight hours. The greenhouse was torn up by the wind and the trees disappeared one night just like the spruce in the "National Forest". The happy ending to the Kotzebue spruce story is that Alaska Airlines shipped in a six foot replacement. We did not try to replace our trees. Losing them was too likely and too traumatic.

Ruth Moline Eddy

An Interesting Life

After a period of adjustment I found my life in the Arctic to be an interesting one. I was certainly not bored. I worked hard almost continually, but that came naturally as part of my German upbringing. My mother was always delighted when she had a productive day – "got a lot done". I was also blessed with abundant energy and recharged quickly. I did not ever feel misused. The workload was not insurmountable, especially since some of our students would drop by to see if there was something they could do. I think some of the attraction was our running water and some of the simple appliances I had, like the toaster, the mixer and the electric wringer washing machine. And they liked to scrub counter tops, and even painted walls.

Some of the older Eskimo women would help by preparing quantities of fish and meat for our use. If I felt a bit of pressure I'd go visit Betty Carr, an elderly Eskimo whose face lit up when anyone crossed the threshold of her tiny wooden house, or go visit any of several sweet older women who were totally positive in their outlook.

ARCTIC CHALLENGE

In the summertime there were Molly and Joe who were always telling me to quit working and come out and enjoy the short summer. They were always good for an anecdote or two.

Of course not everyone was like those I've just mentioned. No, there were those who seemed to make all the wrong choices and we agonized over them. With a few of them we wondered if they would ever change. We did not get angry with them though. We thought of them as being disadvantaged and this made it easier to be patient and not give up. Perhaps we were too sympathetic.

Did we do everything just right in our relationships with the Eskimos and their precious young people? No, we made some mistakes; fortunately not any really serious ones.

One blunder in particular comes to mind. There was a summer celebration for which large heavy picnic tables were carried outdoors from the school basement. Usually the older men did this with a fair amount of exertion. I had a brilliant idea – let the young high school students do the job and surprise these elderly gentlemen by having all the tables out and ready for use, thus sparing them this exhausting physical labor. Wrong way to go! This was their privilege, not their duty. So Edgar, the Eskimo superintendent, let me know he was not pleased. I apologized, of course, but he informed me that Eskimos are not like white men. White men can disagree and then laugh together a few minutes later; Eskimos can not. There was no dog house big enough for me at that point. However, a few days later I found Edgar down in the school basement painting walls – a job that must have seemed quite ridiculous to an Eskimo since Eskimos did not add color to their own houses.

It was one of those times when you realize how effective the teaching of the missionaries had been. Here was a mighty hunter, leader in his village, apologizing through his deeds to a young white woman! It was one of those really humbling experiences. I thanked him in as dignified a manner as I could – and he smiled. Edgar visited us rather frequently after that, and I learned to ASK before I did even kind deeds.

Unfortunately, little Debbie, who was at a very impressionable age, picked up some Eskimo traits. She tended to hold back with other children just like they did with her. This caused her a few problems later on when she enrolled in kindergarten in Michigan. She was very reluctant to speak. I think these white children were just as strange to her as the Eskimo children had once been. She was especially reserved with her teacher who was quite concerned. I don't think Debbie was ready for this very vivacious and outgoing teacher. After the teacher gave her a Samoyed puppy things began to change, and having her over for dinner helped, too. We were so fortunate to have such a caring person to see Debbie through this major adjustment.

I believe that I had just as interesting a social life there as I had back home, perhaps more so. The "white" personnel visited each other frequently and most of them were professional people. Besides, we had many interesting guests. These included anthropologists, sociologists, a team from Scandinavia who crossed the polar ice cap to Kotzebue, military personnel, summer tourists and Lowell Thomas's son.

There were often humorous incidents that kept life interesting. One such incident took place in church. The Eskimo women carried rolls of toilet paper in the pockets of their long parkas to take care of their daily needs and any emergencies. There is a singing group of some kind, usually women, in just about any service. On this particular day the singing group was seated on the platform waiting to perform. One of the women decided to wipe her nose but the roll of toilet paper got away from her. Down the steps of the platform it went, and on down the aisle. She grabbed the paper hoping to pull the roll back but only made it travel faster on its way down the whole length of the church to the front door. Everyone's attention was riveted on the unfolding drama. Most of us were trying desperately not to laugh aloud. The poor woman finally gave in, walked the length of that aisle, picked up the roll, rewound it, tucked it in her pocket and began the long trek up to her place on the platform. Mission Accomplished.

I did see a really angry Eskimo once. It was at the Christmas feast. Someone gave one of the more volatile men a rather smelly tom cod, a small ugly fish, wrapped in brown paper. This was a double insult. First, it was mostly women who caught the tom cod and then this one had seen its better days. The women caught them through holes in the ice in the early spring. It took special equipment and it was a treat to watch their skillful manipulation of ropes and sticks.

Yes, there were some things I missed, like the cleanliness and abundance of the grocery and department stores, and the comforts that those in the lower forty-eight states take for granted. There were also times when I longed for congregational singing that was not loud and nasal. I once consented to singing a duet with another mission worker. The Eskimos were quite intrigued with the difference in sound. They said we sounded like angels. I must admit that neither of us was a great singer, it was just very unlike their robust singing.

ARCTIC CHALLENGE

The midnight sun in Arctic Alaska

Ruth Moline Eddy

ARCTIC CHALLENGE

Wild Creatures of the Arctic

Some of the animals of the Arctic lead a dual life. They are brown like the land in the summer time, white as the snow in winter, and part brown and part white in the spring and fall. These creatures are the snowshoe rabbit, the snowy owl, the Arctic fox, a grouse-like bird called the ptarmigan, and the snow bunting which is a member of the finch family. The snowy owl is an unusual bird in that its eggs begin to incubate as soon as they are laid; therefore the firstborn chick is nearly full grown by the time the last chick hatches. Apparently this is an adaptation to the short summer just as is the rapid development of flowers and seeds in plants.

Then, of course, there is the permanently white king of the Arctic, the polar bear. Because he is so huge and so majestic the bear is the ultimate catch for the avid hunter. Men put their lives and money on the line for one of these. Every year there is speculation among the Eskimos as to who will fare the worst – the bears or the hunters. The Arctic wolf is another grand specimen. We had one mounted who had to be shot because he would not stay away from the village dogs. He was too large to fit on any wall in my current home, so he is on display at a wildlife museum in Bath, Michigan.

Muskrats, ground squirrels and lemmings are small creatures seldom seen except by those who specifically hunt and trap them. Debbie and Jerry's parkas were made from muskrats. Debbie's light-colored one was made from the undersides of the muskrat; Jerry's brown one was made from the backs. Caribou, reindeer and moose were the most useful of all. Their fur and/or hides made clothing and sleeping mats; their meat was delicious, hooves made wonderful sunglasses, the sinew became strong thread, bones would make kitchen tools and needles – there was hardly anything that couldn't be used.

Birds were not too plentiful – ducks were hunted for food – and one year we saw a solitary robin on the ground near our house. Deranged he must have been. We hoped for his sake he wouldn't stay too long. Except for mosquitoes there were few insects and no snakes! Never saw an earthworm, either. The sea abounds with life. Besides the fish, there were seals – wonderful for waterproof clothing, meat and seal oil that was the "Miracle Whip of the Arctic" and could be drunk for warmth and energy. White whales called beluga were a good source of blubber to chew on, also a good source of meat and skins.

ARCTIC CHALLENGE

Stomachs and intestines were used as containers for keeping food, especially berries picked in the summer. Walrus and sea lions could be used much like the seals with the added benefit of ivory tusks for carving and etching and selling to tourists. I have seen bracelets, saltshakers, pickle forks and figurines of all kinds produced by the Eskimos. Most were beautifully crafted.

Speaking of crafting, a popular project for the boys in the shop class was to make a table you could pull chairs up to. Many homes did not have them. The place of honor for a guest was the closest spot to the stove. However, if you had a table your guest could sleep under it, that being one place he was not likely to be stepped on or stumbled over.

There were a number of talented Eskimo artists. One lady named Martha Washington had a very special talent. She made unique Eskimo dolls which were eagerly sought after. She couldn't keep up with the demand. Not only were they beautifully crafted, each doll was the representation of an actual Kotzebue resident. I have a pair and the man was readily identifiable. The female is a mother with a baby tucked over her shoulder inside her parka. When I show these to children there is always an audible "Oh" as I pull out the baby.

Ruth Moline Eddy

Going Home

We were in Kotzebue from July of 1959 to the end of May 1963. School closed on May 17 with an awards assembly and then commencement exercises, a BIA doctor giving the final challenge to the students. It was time to prepare to go home. The next four days consisted of packing our goods in barrels for shipping while talking with those who came to say farewell. Finally a luncheon was given by local merchants, medical workers and our mission associates.

The first step was a flight to Fairbanks to pick up a prearranged car. We were taking a car belonging to the principal of the Kotzebue BIA School (the elementary school) to Seattle for him. He had left it in Fairbanks since there were no roads to Kotzebue. We boarded the plane with mixed emotions. Leaving behind the people who had become our friends and family was not easy. We had never worked so hard nor lived so fully as during our stay in the Arctic. On the other hand we had families we hadn't seen in years, and the welfare of our children to consider.

ARCTIC CHALLENGE

Besides, the third little Moline was due in December.

The trip home was an adventure. We drove down the Alaska Highway (the Canadian part was still unpaved) from Fairbanks to Seattle. We then flew to a friend's home in Oregon, purchased our own car and drove to Michigan. Traveling 4000 miles by car with a two-year-old and a five-year-old was not nearly as hectic as it might sound. There was so much that Jerry, the two-year-old, hadn't seen, like a cow or a horse, a semi trailer truck or a train, a city, a farm or a hundred other things. It was so much fun!

Ruth Moline Eddy

An Update

This nostalgic journey back to Alaska, looking back 40 plus years, has been quite an experience for me. In the year 1990 while I was teaching fourth grade in Durand the class decided they would like to have Eskimo pen pals. We found a fourth and fifth grade teacher in Noorvik who was interested in cooperating in this activity. It was very exciting for my class and very informative for me. From these Eskimo children we were made aware of some of the changes related later in this section.

Since then we have had sporadic contacts with some of our former students. The last one was in 1992 when Don talked to Glen, one of the students who had gone back to his home village of Noorvik and was working as a maintenance man for the schools. Glen had the best of both worlds; he was able to keep many of his Eskimo ways but had added a steady, relatively good-paying job that made it possible for him to have some of the luxuries the "white people" enjoyed. Others went on to school in Anchorage, Oregon, and California. Some went to Fairbanks to live.

ARCTIC CHALLENGE

One joined the Air Force. Another went to the Indian Vocational School (a BIA school) in Kansas, then married and decided to stay in the lower 48. This student went to the BIA school for Indians because he could not afford regular college level studies anywhere else. As an Eskimo he was able to go there free of charge just like the Indians. Eskimos seem to have all the privileges afforded the Indians by the BIA. Eskimos resent being classified with the Indians but the Bureau of Indian Affairs apparently does not differentiate.

The very latest contact with any of the people from that time was made in 1997 when I received a call from a women's auxiliary group asking me to come to Kotzebue to take part in the 100th anniversary of the founding of the first Quaker mission. They had invited three of us who had been involved in the project in Kotzebue. Besides myself they were Janice Perisho, the former teacher, and Huldah Beck, the wife of Harold, the pilot and mission superintendent. All three of us were widowed.

The Eskimo ladies were raising money for our airfare. I had to decline because Jerry's daughter, my first and only granddaughter, was due to be born about that time and I had promised her mother I would be there for her. Her own mother was too ill to fill that role. I have no regrets about that decision. I did write a letter which was read to the thousand or so people assembled at the new, much larger church.

According to the latest information obtained on the Kotzebue web site the town currently has a population of over 3,600. There were 1,200 people in 1959 when we first arrived. Now it has everything a town of this size in mainland USA would boast of, and more. It has a police force, a sanitation department, a fire station, a jail, refuse and recycling services, an animal control system, paved streets and some sidewalks, apartments for seniors, detox centers, and even a college – Chukchi College, a division of the University of Alaska statewide system. Now radio station KOTZ is on the air most, if not all, of the day. Rotman's general store has become a modern attractive combination grocery, variety, and drug store. There is sewage and water service plus a museum with a place for performing arts. As stated earlier, Eskimo continues to be spoken on the streets and in some church services. There are still no roads out of Kotzebue but there are high schools now in almost every village. Students fly to competitions in other villages. The University of Alaska also serves many of its students in their home villages by way of satellite television with fax machines and electronic mail connecting instructors and students.

Copper and iron mining is in full swing in the Kobuk River region. The Red Dog Mine is now reported to be the largest lead and zinc mine in the world. These minerals were always there, but until recently it was too expensive to remove them. Modern technology now makes it profitable. Jade is being removed from what we called Jade Mountain, a hill that shimmered with a green color. The stones occur in various shades of green, brown, black, yellow, white and even red. Gem-quality jade, about one-fourth of the total mined, is used in jewelry making. Jade is the Alaska state gem. I have two shaped and polished chunks of the marbled black, white and green jade from Jade Mountain, brought to us by an Eskimo.

A very important factor in the economic development of Kotzebue, as well as Alaska as a whole, is undoubtedly the revenues generated by the oil industry. In 1982 the state government began to distribute excess funds in the treasury to the residents of the state through a program called the Permanent Fund Dividend Program. Every bona fide resident received a $1,000 payment and these payments have continued every year, in varying amounts, since then.

We could not see all of these changes coming, they were so remarkable, but we knew that in time our students would have to meet progress head-on in a world looking for new frontiers. With this in mind we tried to prepare the young people for contact with the Caucasians who in previous generations had often used the Eskimos so unscrupulously. We worked towards giving them fluency in written and spoken English, to understand finances and business, to have some knowledge of the rest of the world, and to learn how to be responsible workers. In keeping with the goals of the Friends mission we served, we did our best to give the students a foundation in Biblical knowledge as well.

We tried to prepare them in every way possible to meet the new challenges and to develop the confidence needed to enable them to deal with life's difficulties.

Although more remained to be done, with God's help and a strong determination we had met our original challenge. However, before long we were ready for another challenge and embarked on a whole new adventure in a vastly different part of the world. But this will be another story for another time.

Epilogue

Donald Moline, Ruth's husband, fellow teacher and partner in the Arctic adventure, died in 1993 at age 60 of cancer.

Ruth Moline Eddy is retired and lives in Durand, Michigan with her current husband Frank Eddy. Her service in teaching spanned 38 years, beginning in a one-room school in rural Nebraska. Ruth has three children and five grandchildren. In addition to daughter Debbie and son Jerry who were part of this story, there is the youngest son, Wade.

Jerry lives in Greenville, Michigan with his wife, daughter, and stepdaughter and is manager of a Radio Shack store. He is a NASCAR racing enthusiast; perhaps the seeds were planted when watching the dog teams racing. He delighted in seeing the teams disappear into the distance on the Arctic snows.

Debbie, also a teacher, is married and has three sons. She is in no danger from Alaskan huskies where she now lives. She lives in torrid Yuma, Arizona; apparently she is determined to never be cold again.

– the editor

Ruth Moline Eddy